ANATOMY OF SPEED

ANATOMY OF SPEED

INSIDE THE WORLD'S GREAT RACE CARS

TERRY JACKSON

CHARTWELL
BOOKS, INC.

To my parents, Henry and Liz, who brought me up to
believe that there was nothing I couldn't accomplish.

A QUINTET BOOK

Published by Chartwell Books
A Division of Book Sales, Inc.
114 Northfield Avenue
Edison, New Jersey 08837

This edition produced for sale in the U.S.A., its
territories and dependencies only.

ISBN 0-7858-0653-9

This book was designed and produced by
Quintet Publishing Limited
6 Blundell Street
London N7 9BH

Creative Director: Richard Dewing
Designer: Tim Mayer
Project Editors: Katie Preston and Kathy Steer
Editor: Ian Penberthy
Illustrator: Jim Bamber

Typeset in Great Britain by
Central Southern Typesetters, Eastbourne
Manufactured in Singapore by Eray Scan Pte Ltd
Printed in Singapore by
Star Standard Industries (Pte) Ltd

Contents

Introduction

When Michael Schumacher squeezes into the cockpit of his Ferrari Formula One race car, he's wrapping himself in one of the most technologically advanced machines on the face of the planet.

He is surrounded by a carbon fiber tub that is many times stiffer than aluminum, better able to absorb shocks than steel, and is lighter than fiberglass. In the event of a crash, the carbon fiber will shatter in such a way as to dissipate energy away from the cockpit, reducing risk of injury. Despite the high speeds today's drivers race at – over 225 mph is common at the Indianapolis 500 – the use of carbon fiber construction has helped limit the number of life-threatening injuries.

In the side pods are yards of wiring that connects sophisticated electronic devices, which have more computing power than the Apollo spacecraft that took three men to the moon and back. Transmitters relay readings from sensors on all parts of the car to the pit crew, updating data in milliseconds. Accelerometers give readings that can be studied later to determine where on the course Schumacher is fastest, and where he can alter his driving to pick up a critical few tenths of a second. When he pulls into the pits, the readout from a laptop computer provides a guide for getting more speed on the track.

Even the best drivers are only as good as their machines. In 1996, Michael Schumacher has to be patient and work with the engineers at Ferrari on developing the 310T car into a winner.

At his back is a compact 3.0-liter engine that can run at an astounding 16,000 revolutions per minute (rpm) for limited periods to produce upward of 900 horsepower. At peak power, the valves in that engine are opening and closing at a rate of 768,000 times per minute!

The engine power is transmitted through a computer controlled six-speed, semi-automatic gearbox. To shift up, the driver flicks a paddle forward on the steering wheel; to shift down, he pulls back. All the gears are in sequence and a computer automatically adjusts the engine's revolutions to ensure that each shift is smoothly executed within less than a second.

All of this power and technology is wrapped in bodywork that has been developed in the wind tunnel to ensure maximum downforce in the turns, and the least possible drag on the straightaways. Minute, half-degree adjustments to the edges of the front wings can mean the difference between a car that crisply handles a turn and one that goes flying off into the gravel trap. The same is true for the flaps, called wickerbills, at the trailing edges of the rear wings. When it comes to

6

aerodynamics, racing is a game of millimeters. At the sides and underneath the car, air flowing over the body is directed in such a way as to create downforce (literally the ability to push the car to the ground).

Downforce, in concert with the pressure created by the front and rear wings, can hold the modern race car on the track so firmly that drivers like Schumacher routinely experience as much as three times the force of gravity (3g) laterally in high-speed turns.

At such cornering forces, tires play a critical role. Exotic compounds are prepared for every type of racing surface – from rough to smooth, from dry to wet – and pyrometers are used to measure the surface temperatures of the tires to determine if the maximum amount of rubber is being applied in every corner.

Add to all these factors the blend of racing fuel, off-season engineering, pit road technology, the elaborate communications systems between driver and crew, the countless hours spent testing every possible permutation of adjustment, and it's easy to see that the modern race car is nearly as complex as a space shuttle.

Modern design
Although there have been some changes in the last 10 years, the overall look of the modern Formula One race car has remained constant. To the casual observer, this 1987 Camel Team Lotus looks much like a 1996-vintage machine.

When the green flag falls at a race, some may see the spectacle as men in machines that are distant cousins of the family sedan at home. In the days when drivers such as Stirling Moss, Phil Hill, and Juan Fangio competed in the Grand Prix, that link was easy to make. Engines had carburetors, there were no electronics, drivers relied more on "seat-of-the-pants" impressions when testing, and wings were on airplanes.

Now, whether it is the state-of-the-art Formula One machines or the similar, but slightly less advanced, Indycars, most people familiar with auto racing would concede that the car accounts for as much as 95 percent of the winning combination, with the driver making up the remaining 5 percent. That is not to say that a talented driver cannot make a less-than-perfect car a winner. A good example is Jacques Villeneuve, who won the Indycar championship in 1995 before making the jump to Formula One. He took a team that was on the edge of greatness and carried it forward to beat the likes of Roger Penske's formidable organization. Michael Schumacher did much the same with Benetton before being wooed by Ferrari.

Vintage look
Turn the racing history pages back to the early 1960s, such as in this race at Silverstone in England, and you can see how dramatically all aspects of race car construction have changed, from the lack of aerodynamic wings back then to the very skinny tires.

The reality is that race cars have become technologically oriented and even the greatest driver in a less-than-perfect racer cannot win consistently against a lesser competitor in a technically superior car. In Formula One racing, in the world only two or three top teams have the technology to compete for the checkered flag.

In this book, we will examine every aspect and component part that goes into a winning race car in a front-to-back, bolt-by-bolt rundown. When we're through, you'll see why it takes millions of dollars to build a winning car, and why racing is a rolling laboratory for speed.

Race Car Basics

If you could x-ray a modern formula race car and look beneath the skin, your first impression would be that it is as complex as the human body. A tremendous amount of components are arranged under the carbon fiber skin in a manner that makes the best possible use of space and complies with the rules, yet allows the car to function efficiently.

Complex package
Although the modern Formula One car, like this Williams Renault, has very little bodywork, there are a great many technical and aerodynamic wonders at work under the skin.

Under the skin

The nose assembly is attached to the carbon fiber tub, by fittings that allow its quick removal if the nose is damaged during a race. In many cars, the radio transmitter is located in the nose.

The roll bar, which protects the driver if the car flips upside-down in a crash, is a hoop-shaped extension to the rear of the tub. It is also designed to help the flow of air pass cleanly over the car.

The wing assembly normally comprises a combination of wing surfaces and end plates that help direct air flow in such a way as to increase the grip and steering capabilities of the front wheels.

The tires are Goodyear Eagle racing radials, which are available in a variety of rubber compounds that allow the teams to choose the correct grip and wear characteristics for each race track. Each wheel is a three-piece alloy assembly, secured by a single center locking nut.

The shock absorbers (also called dampers) and coil springs ride in an assembly atop the front of the carbon fiber tub. They are connected through pushrods to the A-arm assemblies at the front wheel hub and disc brake assemblies.

Attached to the sides of the carbon fiber tub are pods that contain a variety of equipment. On the left side are the electronic components that gather data from sensors throughout the vehicle and either store the information onboard, or instantly download the data via radio to the pit crew. Also stored in this area of the car are the engine electronics that regulate such features as fuel flow, valve timing, and spark plug firing. On the other side of the car are radiators that remove heat from the engine coolant and oil. The pods also contain ducts that carry air to the radiators, as well as direct airflow in a manner that enhances downforce on the rear wing.

The style of construction used for Formula race cars is called mono-coque. In this, individual components are attached to each other to form the car, rather than being bolted to a separate chassis. The basic component of the monocoque is the tub, which extends from just behind the driver to just forward of his feet.

The overall weight of a Formula One car must be at least 575 kilo-grams (1,268 pounds) without any coolant or lubricants. An Indycar weighs slightly more, with a minimum weight of 1,550 pounds, including the coolant and lubricants.

What about the cost of a Formula One car? It's difficult to estimate, given the development and testing that goes into each one, but a good yardstick is that recently, teams running at the back of the field have been unable to get by on less than $10 million a year. Indycars, because of rules that limit engine, gearbox, and chassis technology, are less expensive. A winning effort can be put together for $7 million per car.

Although there are differences between Formula One cars built by one team or another, the forge of competition – and the Grand Prix rules – tends to dictate similar overall configurations. This cutaway of a Tyrrell reveals how the major components are arrayed.

Behind the driver is the fuel cell, a flexible bladder that is resistant to punctures in a crash. This is separated from the engine and transmission assembly by the tub's rear bulkhead, to which the assembly is bolted. For 1996, the engine size was limited to 3.0 liters, and neither turbo-charging nor supercharging was allowed. The engine is of aluminum alloy and may be a V-8, a V-10, or a V-12. In this case, the engine is a Yamaha V-12.

Behind the engine is the semi-automatic gearbox. Six-speed gearboxes are common, but some Formula One teams have experimented with seven-speed transmissions. The gearbox is linked to an onboard computer that makes shifts at speed without the necessity of a clutch. It is a sequential mechanism, the driver moving a paddle behind the steering wheel up or back to go up or down through the gears. Some cars, like the Tyrrell, retain a clutch for moving from standing, but others have clutchless gearboxes. The driver only has two pedals — gas and brake — situated on the right and left at the front of the tub.

The rear suspension is attached directly to the gearbox, the dampers and springs riding on top of it and being actuated in similar fashion to those at the front. The power is transmitted to the rear wheels through articulated driveshafts – called halfshafts – that run from the back of the gearbox to the rear hub and brake assemblies.

Also attached to the back of the gearbox is the rear wing assembly. As with the front wing, its size and height are governed by the rules, although teams have considerable scope in its configuration. The norm is a wing assembly with full side panels and at least a two-plane horizontal foil that directs air upward at a 60-degree angle. Tiny airfoils at the tip of the wing, called wickerbills, allow precise adjustments to the flow of air.

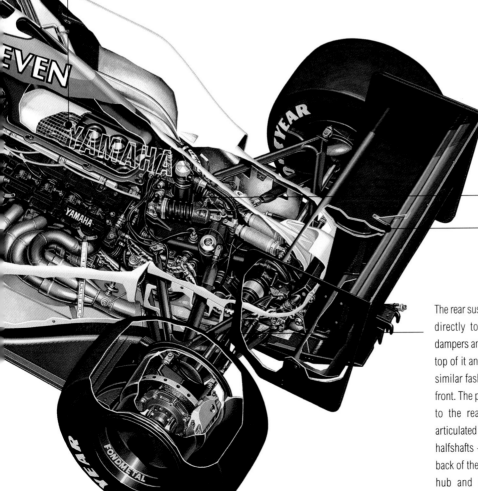

Steering

No matter what goes into a race car, there are certain constants concerning the way it is supposed to perform on the track, particularly in the turns. For any given set of circumstances, a race car may display one of three cornering tendencies: understeer, oversteer, or neutral (the last being the ideal situation that is rarely achieved and sustained throughout a race).

Perfect attitude
Bobby Rahal's Miller Genuine Draft Indycar negotiates a corner in near perfect attitude.

Understeer

As a race car approaches a turn, the driver applies the brakes, then turns the steering wheel. The front wheels don't have enough grip, and the car begins to drift to the outside of the turn. In a severe case of understeer, the car would never turn properly, and the racer would shoot off the course. To control understeer, more grip is needed at the front wheels, and this can be achieved in several ways. The driver can apply the brakes, which would shift weight to the front, providing more downforce on the front tires. He can also apply more power and cause the rear end to kick out, realigning the car's direction. Or he can ask the crew to adjust the front wing to provide more aerodynamic downforce at the front wheels. Through the use of acceleration and braking, a car that displays slight understeer can be controlled. If you're a fan of NASCAR, you'll often hear drivers saying that their cars are "pushing," which is another way of describing understeer.

Oversteer

In this case, the front wheels have plenty of grip, but the rear wheels lose traction. Less predictable than understeer, oversteer can be caused by an imbalance in the front-rear brake bias, worn rear tires, or improperly adjusted wings. Unlike understeer, which normally occurs gradually, oversteer can happen quickly and without much warning to the driver. Uncorrected, it will cause the rear end to swing completely around and send the car into an uncontrolled spin. One way to correct oversteer is to use opposite lock – turning the wheels in the direction of the spin, and applying power to shift weight back to the rear wheels. A few drivers prefer a car in which a little oversteer can be induced by the throttle – they enter a turn, then stand on the gas, bringing the back end out in a controlled slide. It's a crowd-pleasing way through a turn, but it is rarely the fastest way around a track.

Oversteer
Robby Gordon's Walker Racing Indycar exhibits
classic oversteer.

Understeer
Benetton Formula One machine pushes toward the outside of a
turn, which is usually caused by understeer.

The racing line

If you were to examine a race track and analyze each turn for the fastest way around, eventually you would identify what racers call "the line." Simply put, the line is the best way to enter a turn, cut its apex, then exit at the highest possible speed onto the next straightaway. As you watch a race, you'll see drivers set themselves up for a turn at the outside edge of the track, sweep through to briefly touch the inside curbing of the turn, then accelerate out to the outer edge of the pavement and down the straight.

The line is easily recognized at most race tracks: it's the darker area of the pavement where the continual passage of race cars has left a trail of rubber. Follow the correct line through each turn, and you will be guaranteed a smooth lap. The trick, however, is understanding that the line varies for each type of turn. If all turns were constant-radius left-hand bends, figuring out the line would be simple. But many turns have different angles; sometimes there are two apexes in the same long, sweeping turn. There are the esses – quick left-right bends that toss the car from side to side. Then there are hairpins, turns so sharp that race cars slow to a crawl and hug the inside to get safely around.

Compounding the problem for drivers is that *everyone* on the track wants to be on the line, so to pass you've got to find the next-fastest way around the turn and hope that your machine can "out muscle" the other guy.

Perfect line
David Coulthard, in a Williams, cuts a perfect line through some esses.

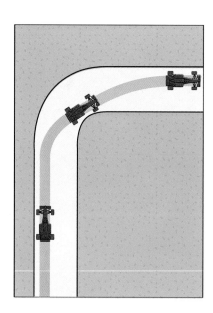
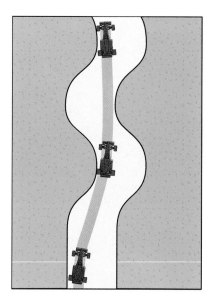

Off line

A Williams Renault is off the line and way up on a curb. This is what happens when a driver miscalculates and misses the correct line through a turn, cutting the apex too closely.

Nose-to-tail

A McLaren Honda leads a pack of cars through a turn at Monza. Because there is normally only one line through a turn, passing is difficult. As a result, cars will often go through turns nose-to-tail, glued to the fast line.

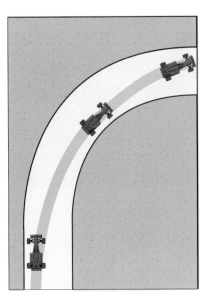
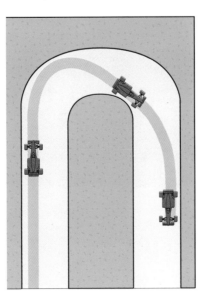

The best way through a turn

These diagrams show the best way for a driver to attack a variety of turns on a race track. At the far left, a simple but tight right-hander requires the driver to sweep to the inside of the turn, touch the apex and then power out to the edge of the track. In a series of ess turns, the goal is to plot as straight a line as possible that just clips the apex of each bend. In a high-speed right-hander, little or no braking is needed, just a smooth arc. One way through a sharp 180-degree bend is to brake late, turn sharply and then accelerate through the apex in a straight line.

Passing

Because the racing line at most race tracks is so narrow, most passing occurs at the end of long straightaways using several techniques. One of these is called drafting which has become more difficult as race cars have made greater use of aerodynamic aids. In its most basic form, drafting involves one car tucking up behind another at high speed. The car in front cuts through the air for the second car, the engine of which doesn't have to work as hard to achieve the same speed.

Let's say that the lead car's engine was turning at 10,000 rpm down the straight. The second car, which doesn't have to face the same wind resistance, can keep up by running at only 9,500 rpm. It has some power in reserve to pull out and pass the lead car at the end of the straight. Sometimes, two cars locked up in a draft can move faster than one car because of the larger envelope they create in the atmosphere.

You will often see one car pass another by pulling up on it, gaining a tow from the draft, then ducking to the inside of the lead car at the end of the straight. Once this was a classic passing maneuver, and it still is on the NASCAR circuit. But the aerodynamics of Formula One and Indycar designs have made it more difficult. As air spills off the rear wings of an open-wheeled car, it is often turbulent. That turbulent air can disrupt the downforce of a trailing car because it doesn't pass cleanly over the front wings. So while a trailing car may enjoy a horsepower advantage due to drafting, the driver could find that its handling in the turns will be disrupted.

A common passing method is to out-brake an opponent when entering a turn. A driver waits a little longer than his opponent before braking for a turn, then darts in front and forces the other car off line or makes them fall in behind. Performed correctly, it's the best way around a car with similar straight-line performance. Brake too late, and the car won't make the turn; it will fly off the track or crash.

Outbraking

A common method of passing is to out-brake your opponent. Here, the cars dive for the first corner at the start of a race. The driver who waits until the last possible moment to brake will win the duel.

Late braking

Trying to take a turn under braking can have disastrous consequences, as this scene at the Argentine Grand Prix shows. By waiting too long to brake, one car bumps another.

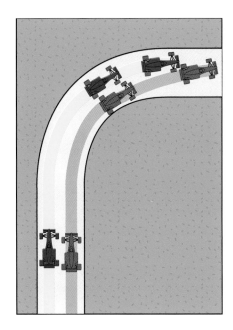

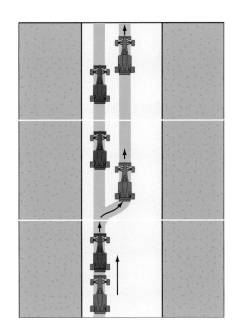

Braking

This shows a classic pass under braking. The pursuing car waits until the lead car starts to brake for a turn, then dives inside before braking. If all goes well, the overtaking car will be able to claim the corner and force the competitor to take a slower line through the turn. If the pursuing car miscalculates, however, it will push to the outside of the turn after the apex, and the competitor will be able to retake the lead on the exit of the turn.

Drafting

The envelope of air that opens up for a trailing car when drafting begins between 20 and 75 feet behind the leading car in Formula One racing. The rear wings of the car in front can create air turbulence for the pursuing car if it gets too close. In NASCAR, where the aerodynamic aids are much more restricted, cars can draft right up to the lead car's rear bumper.

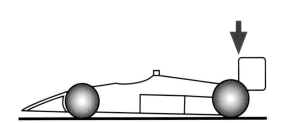

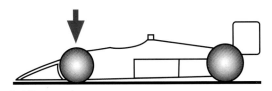

Getting a grip

Under braking, the weight of the car shifts from the back to the front. The wings on the car help maintain the downforce at both the front and the back so that the tires maintain maximum contact with the road and slow the car faster.

Lined up

Coming down a long straight at Monza in 1991, many of the cars are lined up, one behind another, drafting. As they approach the turn, an overtaking car can pull out and gain some speed because it has not had to force its way through the atmosphere.

17

Pit stops

Another way for a race driver to get ahead of an opponent is in the pits. Pit stops have long been a fixture in US races, and in recent years have been added to Formula One races. Rather than carry enough fuel to go the distance in a race, cars generally carry only enough for about 100 miles. Also, softer compound tires have become the norm to improve traction and cornering, and they tend to lose their grip as the race wears on. Thus, pit stops where the fuel tank is filled and four tires replaced are common in most forms of racing.

The difference of just a few seconds in the time spent in the pits can give a race car a considerable lead on the track, or evaporate a lead that a driver has worked hard to establish.

The way that pit stops are accomplished varies greatly from one form of racing to another. In Formula One, for instance, the pit lane often looks like a crowded bazaar, since the rule makers have not set any limits on the number of people who can work on a car when it comes in. Indycar, by contrast, limits the number of workers beyond the pit wall to

Large crew
This Ferrari pit stop shows the major difference between Indycar and Formula One. As many people as necessary can work on the car when it pulls in. The result is that a perfect stop can take less than 10 seconds, compared to about 18 seconds for an Indycar stop.

Pit control
This person indicates with a sign on a long pole exactly where the driver should stop. Once stopped, the control person holds the sign in front of the cockpit to indicate that work is still being done. When work is complete and all crew members are clear, the sign is flipped over and the word "GO" is shown on the other side, a signal that the driver can take off.

Driver's aid
This person has responsibility for attending to any problems the driver may have a dirty visor, the need for a quick drink from a squeeze bottle, or a tightening of the safety belts.

Jack men
One person fore and aft who have levered jacks that fit to portions of the suspension when the car pulls in. The jacks are connected up and then the bottom, the jacks are rotated so that the car is raised 12 inches off the ground. When service is down, both jacks are dropped and the car is away.

Refueler
A two-person job. One person in a full fire suit and helmet attaches the hose, which uses a special coupler, to the large inlet on the car behind the driver. The second person helps with the hose and works a vent hose that helps the fuel flow faster into the tank.

Tire changes
In Formula One, there are at least two and sometimes three people per wheel. One person uses the pneumatic wrench to loosen the single wheel nut, another pulls off the old tire, and a third slaps the new tires into place and the man with the wrench reattaches the wheel nut.

Indy crews
An Indycar pit crew goes to work, changing all four tires and filling the tank with 20 gallons of methanol. Indycar rules allow only six people over the pit wall, so tire changers must do one side of the car, then run to the other side to complete the work.

six at any one time, as does NASCAR. Also, in an effort to avoid repeating accidents that have killed pit workers, Indycar and NASCAR impose speed limits on the pit road, and mandate that all refueling must be by gravity feed. There are higher speed limits in Formula One, and pressurized refueling rigs are standard. The result is that Formula One pit stops are very quick – often less than 10 seconds for fuel and four tires.

The key to a quick stop is choreography. On a Formula One stop, as many as 18 people swarm over the car, each with a specific task. There are three people per wheel – one to remove the locking nut, another to remove the old tire, and a third to roll in the new tire. Two people handle the fueling rig. One person at each end operates a manual jack; one person stands by with a starter in case the engine stalls; and another holds a sign paddle in front of the driver telling him when it's safe to go.

In Indycar, there is one person for each tire, one person with the fuel line, and one person who inserts a pneumatic hose that activates two jacks in the car. With less manpower and a gravity feed for the fuel, an Indycar stop can take 18 seconds or longer.

Jack man
A NASCAR pit stop generally follows the same rules as an Indycar stop. The only difference is that there is a man who handles a conventional frame jack to raise the car, as opposed to the built-in pneumatic system used to raise Indycars. In NASCAR, the jack man must run from one side of the car to the other in unison with the tire changers.

Speed stop
Team McLaren executes a speedy pit stop. Until recently, pit stops were unusual in Formula One. Then the rules were changed to limit the amount of gasoline a car can carry, forcing teams to choreograph quick pit stops.

Suspension and Chassis

As important as a powerful engine is to a modern race car, suspension design and tuning often surpass raw horsepower as the final step to the winner's podium. The suspension – defined here as the mechanical and structural parts of a race car that link the wheels and tires to the vehicle – allows a race car to negotiate turns rapidly. And in all forms of circuit racing, the battle is won in the turns.

G Forces
Where Formula One cars have been able to make vast speed improvements is in their ability to go faster in corners, sometimes developing more than 3 G's of cornering force.

Front suspension

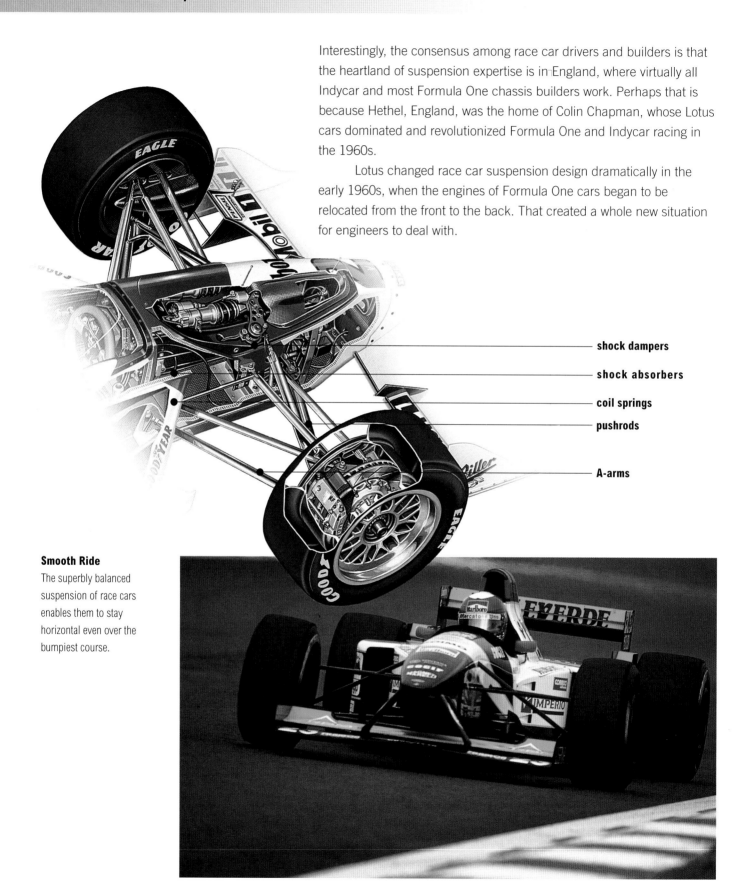

Interestingly, the consensus among race car drivers and builders is that the heartland of suspension expertise is in England, where virtually all Indycar and most Formula One chassis builders work. Perhaps that is because Hethel, England, was the home of Colin Chapman, whose Lotus cars dominated and revolutionized Formula One and Indycar racing in the 1960s.

Lotus changed race car suspension design dramatically in the early 1960s, when the engines of Formula One cars began to be relocated from the front to the back. That created a whole new situation for engineers to deal with.

—— shock dampers

—— shock absorbers

—— coil springs

—— pushrods

—— A-arms

Smooth Ride
The superbly balanced suspension of race cars enables them to stay horizontal even over the bumpiest course.

An engine in the rear provided better weight distribution and virtually eliminated what is called "polar movement." To visualize polar movement, link two tennis balls with string and throw them into the air. They will usually start to rotate and, but for the force of gravity that pulls them to the ground, they would probably continue to rotate.

Spinning out

In the front-engined cars of the 1950s and earlier, the weight of the engine up front and location of the driving wheels at the rear would create a polar movement when a car entered a turn. It would often start to turn and, if unchecked, would continue until it began to loop or spin out. With the engine at the rear, polar movement was reduced considerably.

Another benefit of moving the engine was that it removed the need for beefy front suspensions that not only had to negotiate turns, but also had to bear the weight of the engine. A more graceful and precise arrangement evolved and today almost all open-wheeled racers – particularly Formula One and Indycar – use the same type of suspension, known as the wishbone or A-arm setup.

Reynard Suspension
You can clearly see the A-arm suspension assembly on this 1996 Reynard chassis.

Optimum control

At first sight, the front suspension of an open-wheeled race car looks far too spindly to support it, much less hold the tires precisely to the pavement in the turns without snapping or bending. Yet all of the front suspension parts work in concert to absorb the pounding on the track and give the driver optimum steering control.

At the front of a typical Formula One or Indycar, the wheels are connected at each side by wide suspension members called A-arms (wishbones). The name derives from their shape – the tip of the "A" connects to the wheel hub, while the feet are linked to the car's tub. There is an A-arm at the top and one at the bottom. There are two types of A-arm suspension – equal-length and unequal-length. A suspension where the A-arms at top and bottom are identical in length is an equal-length setup. Where the sizes differ, it is unequal-length. The geometry of these setups determines how the wheels and tires ride over the road.

Internal mountings

Unlike a street car, the shock absorbers and springs do not ride out near the wheel. Instead, a pushrod runs from the lower edge of the hub assembly up to the shocks and springs, which are mounted in the car's nose. In front of the A-arms and shock pushrod are the steering arms, which connect to a steering knuckle also inside the car's nose. All of the pieces are made of hollow aluminum or carbon fiber for maximum strength, yet lightweight.

The modern A-arm design

Pushrod link

The shock absorbers and springs are situated in the nose of the modern open-wheeled race car, and are connected to the hubs by pushrods. When the wheel moves up or down, that motion is passed through the pushrod, which connects to a bell crank (center) that is linked to the spring and shock. The springs and shocks are quite stiff, allowing very little movement. The result is a harsh ride, but the tires stay on the ground. Teams can vary the suspension setup by changing the springs, which are tuned for different levels of stiffness.

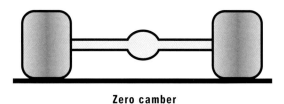

Zero camber

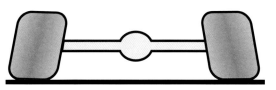

Negative camber

Camber

A race car's stance on the road differs greatly from a street car because of camber. Camber refers to the angle a car's wheels and tires make in relation to the pavement. At rest, the wheels on a street car are perpendicular to the road. On a race car, the camber is set so that the wheels are tipped inward slightly. This ensures that when the car moves through the range of turns, it tracks more easily, and the maximum amount of tread is on the ground through the turns, where the greatest grip is needed.

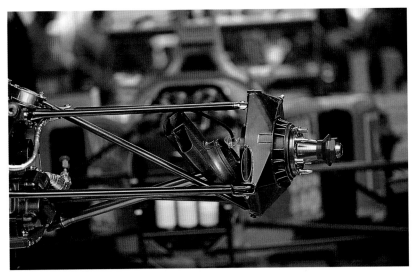

Cooling duct
Another view of the front suspension, this time showing the addition of a small duct to sweep cooling air to the brakes.

Universal feature
The front suspension of a McLaren shows how the A-arm design is accepted universally. However, small changes in spring stiffness, and other adjustments, can make a big difference to how a car handles.

Hub connection
The A-arm suspension on this 1996 Reynard Indycar chassis connects to the wheel hub, which also carries the disc brake assembly.

Shock absorbers

Shock absorbers – called dampers by most race car designers – are finely-tuned pieces of the front and rear suspension. As in a passenger car, they are designed to cushion road bumps or severe movement on the wheels. But unlike in a passenger car, the shocks are set to much stiffer tolerances and are designed to react far more quickly and precisely than street car shock absorbers. The shocks on most Formula One cars ride inside coil springs that also help limit suspension travel. The shocks act on the suspension through a bellcrank and pushrod assembly that attaches to the wheel hub. The internal shock pressure, which determines its stiffness, can be adjusted, and the coil springs also can be changed to alter a car's handling characteristics.

Compact design
The shocks rest compactly inside the coil springs on this Formula One car. The reservoir is out of sight in the nose of the car.

Sophisticated system
A more complex reservoir flow arrangement is used on this Formula One car.

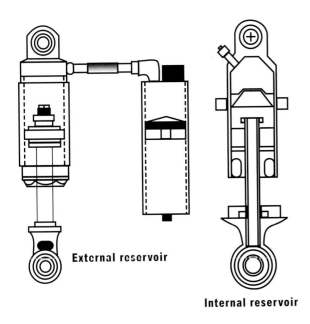

External reservoir

Internal reservoir

How it works

Here is an example of how an external-reservoir shock absorber works. As the piston inside the shock moves upward, it compresses oil in the tube above, which restricts its movement. When the damper can no longer move against the oil, it starts its rebound stroke, and the oil expands. The exterior reservoir allows a more compact shock design and also easy adjustment of the pressure within the shock. The higher the pressure, the stiffer the shock.

Making adjustments

Engineers for the Team Green Indycar effort work at the nose of their 1996 Reynard chassis in the area where the external reservoir for the shock absorbers would normally be installed.

External reservoir

Shock absorbers on a race car differ from a street car in several aspects. Most, like these on a 1996 Reynard, have an external reservoir for the gas or oil that damps the piston motion inside the shock. The advantage is that the reservoir pressure can be adjusted to correct the firmness of the shock absorbers.

Carbon fiber

What has also changed the face of racing is the use of composite materials, such as carbon fiber and Kevlar, in chassis construction. These immensely strong, but lightweight, materials were initially developed as part of the space program. Similar in construction to fiberglass – it's made by bonding fibers together in an overlay pattern – carbon fiber can be found throughout a race car. The advantages of carbon fiber are that it is very lightweight and rigid, yet it can be worked into complex rounded forms like the tub and bodywork of a race car.

The use of carbon fiber also means that suspensions don't have to support so much weight and can be pared down to very spidery proportions. The result is that the chassis and suspension of a race car look very fragile, yet are strong enough to withstand the stresses of competing at speeds of 200 mph.

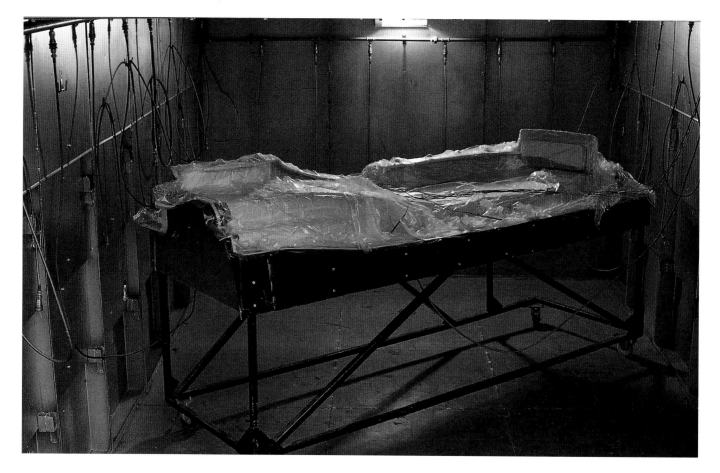

Building a carbon fiber tub
A movable frame is used to support the finished bucks (mock-ups) while the resin and carbon fiber bodyshell is built. It is a multistep process that involves using several different materials to achieve a body that is both lightweight and strong, which will withstand the downforce and lateral g-forces on the race track.

A strong monocoque

This sidepod floor shows how honeycombed aluminum and carbon fiber are used to form a strong, yet light, basis for the main monocoque components on a 1996 Reynard.

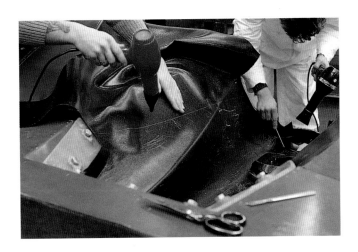

Applying the sheeting

Workers using heat guns apply the carbon fiber sheeting over the resin body panels.

Final trimming

A nose and cockpit section of a Lola after it has been trimmed and made ready for assembly.

A life saver

Carbon fiber is lighter than aluminum, yet many times stronger. It is, however, very brittle and in a crash tends to shatter rather than bend. This is a benefit, though, because as it shatters, it helps dissipate the energy of the impact. In a serious accident, this can even save the driver's life. Without carbon fiber and other composite materials, today's race cars would not be nearly so safe.

The chassis designers try to create a car where everything but the cockpit – called the survival cell – can tear away in the event of a crash. The cockpit is built so that it will keep debris from piercing the area around the driver, as well as keeping the driver from contact with the pavement. Starting in 1996, Formula One rules makers mandated even more improvements to the cockpit survival cell to further minimize the chance of injury.

Protective tub

Rubens Barrichello's crash in a turn at Imola shows how sturdy, yet safe, a carbon fiber monocoque can be. He gets airborne and hits the tire wall, but the basic tub of the car remains intact, protecting Barrichello from life-threatening injury.

Dissipating energy

One of the safety advantages of carbon fiber is that in a crash it helps dissipate energy away from the driver. When the nose and sidepod of this McLaren were ripped away in a crash, it undoubtedly looked like a life-threatening accident to spectators. In reality, however, the more a car sheds pieces in a crash — so long as the main tub remains intact — the safer the driver is. Very simply put, as each piece breaks away, it carries with it some of the energy of the impact, energy that doesn't reach the driver.

31

Chassis evolution

In the 1950s, most race cars – as well as most street cars – had a ladder-type frame that formed the basis for the chassis. The body was mounted on the frame as a separate unit. Although strong, it was a heavy assembly that restricted suspension movement. This form of construction was eventually replaced by the monocoque design, in which the actual body of the race car was made strong enough for the engine, transmission, and suspension to be bolted directly to it, and there was no need for a separate frame. The result was less sprung weight on the suspension, which improved handling immensely.

The ladder frame
The ladder frame uses two or more stout side rails held together by several cross-members – hence its relationship to a fireman's ladder.

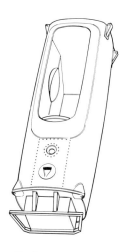

Early monocoques
Lotus was one of the first Formula One teams to develop the monocoque design, in which the body of the car – in this case, the tub where the driver sits – becomes an integral part of the chassis. Other components, such as the suspension, engine, and transmission, are hung off of the monocoque.

Design dinosaur
In its day, the 1969 Lotus 49B was on the cutting edge of Formula One technology. Now, with its cigar-shaped cockpit and its modest aerodynamics, it looks positively simple.

Aerodynamic aid
Once the monocoque design became the racing industry's standard, other avenues were explored to improve handling. The Lotus Type 79 was one of the first to adopt modern aerodynamic theory, and it proved a near unbeatable car in its day.

Modern approaches
This 1996 Tyrell uses a variety of aerodynamic devices, such as diffusers and wings that direct the airflow around and over the body, to help generate downforce. Although the rules restrict the use of full ground effects to create a vacuum under the car, considerable downforce is generated through these other means.

Rear suspension

At the rear, the suspension is hung off the transmission, which is the rearmost part of the chassis. A-arms are also employed at the back to control wheel movement. The configuration of the A-arms and the links to the shock absorbers, together with the stiffness of the coil springs, combine to keep that movement to a minimum.

It sounds pretty simply, and in theory it is. However, the key to building a winning race car is designing the suspension parts and tuning them once assembled so that they provide optimum control and response in every turn – whether it is a tight left-hander, a sweeping right-hander, or a series of ess curves.

It's a science that has been honed ever sharper through competition.

Side view
A side view of the rear suspension in a McLaren Honda in France during 1989.

Strong arms

The A-arm design that is used on the front suspension is carried over to the rear of the car, as in this 1996 Reynard chassis. The arms are beefier, however, because of the greater stresses imposed by the engine on this part of the suspension.

Suspension geometry

This rear view of a McLaren clearly shows the geometry of the rear suspension, and the method of mounting the rear wing to the gearbox and chassis.

Load-bearing gearbox

The rear suspension is literally hung off the gearbox which, in a monocoque design, becomes a load-bearing member of the chassis. In a conventional road car, the rear suspension A-arms would be mounted to a frame, as would the rear driveshafts and differential.

Halfshafts and shock links

This rear shot of a Yamaha-powered Tyrrell shows how the halfshafts run from the gearbox to the rear wheels. You can also see the suspension pushrods that connect the shock absorbers and springs, at the top of the gearbox, to the rear hub assembly.

Shocks, springs, and A-arms

If the rear suspension of a race car seems complex, that's because it has to be. Consider what happens when a rear tire moves over a bump on the track (and most race tracks are not mirror smooth, though they may look that way on TV). The wheel moves up and over the bump, which causes the chassis to react. If the spring allows the chassis to continue moving upward, it can pull the tire off the ground, resulting in a loss of traction. The trick is to tune the rear suspension so it is stiff enough to keep the tire on the road, but soft enough to prevent the whole car from jumping sideways whenever a bump is encountered. In addition, allowance must be made for the vertical movement of the suspension during braking, acceleration, and cornering, so you can see why chassis engineers work long and hard to discover the ideal combinations, then keep them closely-guarded secrets.

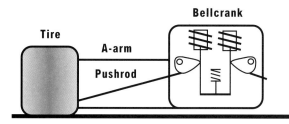

Typical rear suspension

Ride height adjustment

Keeping the ride height constant is a key to handling and aerodynamics, and one way in which that is done is through the use of a third spring and a bump stop that regulates how far down the suspension can be compressed.

Stronger components

As the rear wings become more complex – this car has a three-plane rear wing – the downforce on the rear suspension becomes greater. This means that the rear A-arms are subject to a much higher loading than the front A-arms. Therefore, the rear arms on most race cars are much thicker in diameter.

Complex design
Another view of the rear suspension, showing its complexity.

Restricted travel
As with the front suspension, the shock absorbers are mounted inboard from the rear wheels and are connected by pushrods to the rear hubs. The pushrods react to movement of the rear wheels, passing that motion to the coil springs and shock absorbers. These are tuned to allow only a very small amount of travel in the rear suspension.

Tires

Today's race cars are faster through the turns, and handle better than any open-wheeled vehicles before them. One reason for this is the tremendous leap in tire technology that has occurred over the past 10 years. Although diameter and width vary, most Formula One race tires are 13 inches in diameter and about 16 inches across. They are of radial design in the underlying carcass, and the compound on the footprint of the tire is often varied from track to track. At most venues, Goodyear – the number one supplier in the world – will bring as many as three compounds (typically designated "A," "B," and "C," which will vary in softness, the "C" compound usually being the softest. What teams try to achieve is a compromise between softness, which translates into more grip, and tire wear. The softer the tire, the more it wears.

Next to fuel, tires are the most expendable commodity at a race track. In an effort to reduce costs, the Formula One regulations set limits on how many sets of tires a team can use in a weekend. NASCAR and Indycar have similar rules.

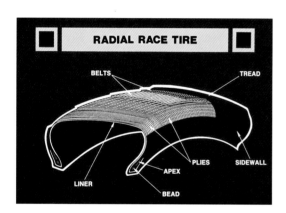

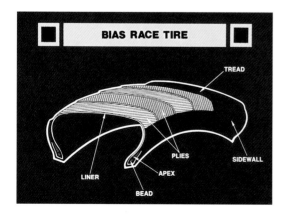

Radial versus bias-ply

These two diagrams show the difference in construction between a bias-ply tire and a radial tire. By its design, a radial tire has better road-grip characteristics because the sidewall flexes more, while the footprint – the part of the tire that is on the road – stays put. The problem in developing race tires was in constructing a radial that could withstand the extreme side loadings and not abruptly break traction when at the limit. Bias-ply tires, which have less flexible sidewalls, were more predictable at the limits of cornering. By the late 1980s, however, engineers had perfected a radial design that provided greater roadholding capabilities, yet was more predictable in how it reacted in corners.

Rain tires

The other type of tire that is used in Formula One and some types of Indycar racing is the rain tire. For most people, these tires appear to be more familiar, since there are many passenger car tires – most notably Goodyear's Gatorback sports car tire – that have a similar tread pattern. In fact, high-performance street radials are a direct offshoot of Formula One rain tire design. The tread pattern helps sweep water out from under the tread to maintain maximum possible contact with the racing surface. When the track dries out, however, these tires would wear too quickly because of heat buildup caused by tread wiggle. As the tread blocks move, the tires become hotter. High temperatures can break down the rubber and cause the tire to fail. A normal racing slick is less prone to heat buildup because it has no tread blocks. But in the wet, water will collect under a slick, causing the car to aquaplane – lose contact with the road – and the driver will have no control.

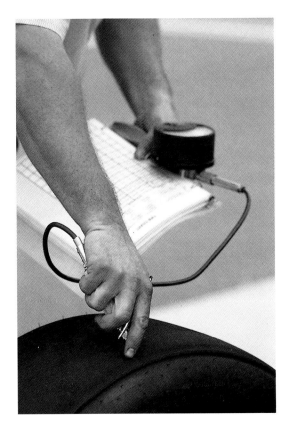

Measurements

Once the tires are on the car, engineers take several different measurements to discover how they are performing. Using a pyrometer, an engineer checks the temperatures on the face of the tire immediately it comes into the pits during testing. Measurements are taken at three points across the face, and for most tracks the temperatures shouldn't vary by more than 5 degrees across the face. If they do, it might indicate that the suspension is causing one part of the tire to do more work than the others, which would increase wear during a race. Engineers also check total tire circumference when the tire is at race temperature. Nitrogen, rather than oxygen, is used to inflate the tires because it is less prone to expansion when heated. Just a few millimeters in tire expansion can change a car's handling characteristics. In fact, most teams vary the circumference from one side to another – called stagger – to improve handling on some courses, especially ovals.

Major supplier

This rear Formula One tire is made by Goodyear, the number one supplier of race tires in the world.

Skinny tires

These are vintage Formula One machines; note how skinny the tires are.

Active Suspension

In the late 1980s, Formula One teams began to experiment with active suspensions. Using computers and super fast sensors, teams were designing spring and shock absorber systems that could alter the suspension setup, while the car was in motion, to match its speed, the turn, road surface, and braking. The results were dramatic: Williams cars were the clear leaders at many tracks because of their active suspensions.

However, the systems came in for severe criticism. There were gripes that with active suspensions, race cars really didn't need talented drivers. A machine was doing all the work that once was left to the driver to handle. Then there was the cost. The development of software and other components was phenomenally expensive, and only the top teams – Williams, McLaren, and Ferrari – had budgets that could support such work. It further split the big-budget teams (with $100 million annually to spend) from the less well-off operations, which make do with just $25 million a year.

As a result, starting in 1993, Formula One officials banned active suspensions, returning some control to the drivers. So how did the technology work? Most teams kept it a closely-guarded secret, but these photographs show what appear to be electronic switches that regulate the pressure in the spring dampers, as well as other items that are unexplained.

Typical race car active suspension

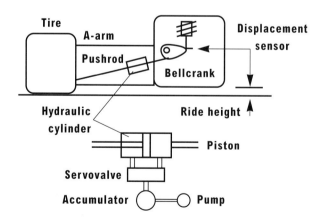

Active suspension

Here is one possible scenario for how an electronically controlled active suspension could work. A hydraulically activated piston is used along the pushrod, and the pressure in the piston is regulated by sensors that measure ride height, lateral forces, shock movement and wheel position. The sensor then adjusts the piston pressure to meet the demands of constantly changing road conditions.

The 1995 McLaren front suspension.

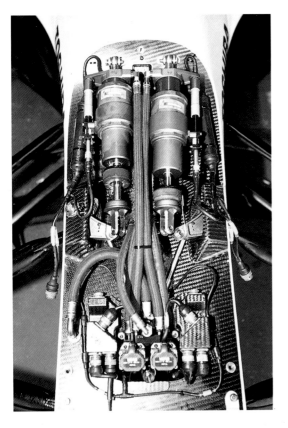

1993 active suspension at Monza, Italy.

The McLaren active suspension system in the 1992
Formula One car.

1995 Williams.

Classic Battles

3

In the days before sponsorship became such a vital part of auto racing, teams represented nationalities, and it was a battle between the Italians and the Germans, the British and the Americans. Now, with cars covered in decals rather than their national colors, fans root for drivers and teams. They also have their favorite chassis marques.

Robby Gordon in a Valvoline Indycar is one of the new competitors in Indycar who has been knocking at the door of success against seasoned veterans like Michael Andretti and Al Unser Jr.

Formula One versus Indy

To most people, a Formula One car and an Indycar look nearly identical. The wheels have no fenders, the suspension parts look similar, the driver sits in about the same spot, the engine and transmission look similar and are in the same general positions. But in many ways Formula One cars and Indycars are very different. Here are some key points:

Transmission

Formula One technology has surpassed Indycar when it comes to gearboxes. Semi-automatic transmissions eliminate the traditional clutch and manual shift method of changing gears. Now a computer controls engine speed when changing gear, instantly selecting the right gear when the driver actuates a paddle on the steering column. In Indycar, the gearboxes have straight-cut gears and changes are slower. Although the Indycar has a clutch, drivers shift up and down through the gears without the clutch by regulating engine speed with the gas. The clutch is almost always used for getting away from a standing start. Both Indycar and Formula One gearboxes have six speeds, although some Formula One teams have experimented with seven-speed.

Sidepods and underside

Two ways in which Formula One and Indycars differ is in the onboard electronic telemetry that is allowed, and in the amount of ground effects the chassis underside is permitted to generate. When it comes to electronics, there are no restrictions in Formula One, so cars have a vast array of sensors and transmitters that send data to the pits during a race. This allows the teams to monitor the car's handling dynamics in every turn, to determine instantly what is going on in the engine and gearbox, and to prepare to make changes when the car comes in. In Indycar racing, data acquisition is largely limited to engine performance. On the underside, Indycars aren't allowed to use ground effect tunnels; the car must have a flat bottom. Formula One is moving in this direction, dictating flat bottoms and ride height minimums.

Engine

In the Formula One car, the engine is limited in size to 3.0 liters, down from the 3.5-liter limit of a few years ago, and is normally aspirated. The latter means that no turbochargers are allowed to force air into the engine. Otherwise, engine technology is wide open, and teams spend millions on developing their engines. There are V-8s, V-10s, and V-12s on the Formula One circuit. In Indycars, the size is limited to 2.65 liters, but the engines are turbocharged. V-8 designs are universal and, unlike Formula One, the teams don't own their engines. Engines are developed and built by an outside supplier — Ilmor, Honda, Ford, Toyota — then leased to the teams. They are not allowed to make any modifications to the engines, but some teams enjoy close relationships with their suppliers and often benefit from the latest developments in engine technology.

FORMULA ONE VERSUS INDY

Here is a rundown on how the 1996 versions of these cars compare.

	Formula One	Indycar
Construction:	Carbon fiber and composites	Carbon fiber and composites
Weight:	600kg (1,320 pounds)	704.5kg (1,550 pounds)
	Includes driver and fluids	Includes fluids, not driver
Brakes:	All carbon and composite discs, pads, calipers. No ABS	Cast-iron discs, carbon pads, composite calipers. No ABS
Engine:	3-liter maximum: 12 cylinders maximum. Must be four-cycle internal combustion. No rotary pistons. No turbocharging or supercharging	Turbocharged V-8: DOIIC with a maximum of 2.65 liters. Turbocharged pushrod maximum of 209.3 inches. 366-cubic-inch non-turbo engines also allowed
Gearbox:	Semi-automatic transmissions allowed. No fully automatic gearboxes allowed	No semi- or fully automatic gearboxes allowed
Fuel:	Regulations call for "pump" gasoline of between 92 and 102 RON	Methanol is mandatory. Methanol is a man-made fuel based on alcohol
Ground effects:	Banned. Rules limit the amount of downforce	Banned. Rules limit the amount of downforce
Traction control:	Once permitted, now banned	Never allowed
Active suspension:	Once permitted, now banned	Never allowed

Fuel

Both types of car use inflatable fuel bladders that are encased in separate rigid cells to minimize the possibility of leakage in a crash, which could cause a fire. However, the two types differ in what fills those fuel tanks. The Formula One cars run on ultra-high-octane gasoline, while the Indycars use methanol, an alcohol-based fuel. Formula One fuel tends to be very exotic and, at one point, teams were running very volatile blends, often using one for qualifying and another for the race itself. The cost of these fuels was enormous, and not all fuels were available to all teams. So the FIA stepped in and mandated one gasoline standard, although some teams were disqualified in early races for infractions of the rules. In Indycar racing, the methanol has the same rating as high-grade racing gas, but it is safer because it is less prone to explosion in a crash. One drawback is that methanol burns with a clear flame, so a pit fire can develop without being seen. An advantage, however, is that water will quickly douse the flames.

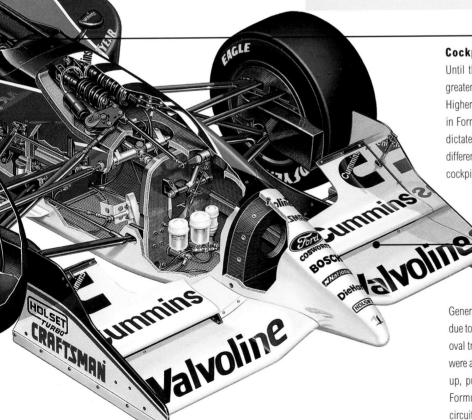

Cockpit

Until the 1996 season, Indycar cockpits were designed with a greater degree of driver protection than Formula One cockpits. Higher side coaming and padding were the rule in Indycar, while in Formula One, the driver was more exposed. For 1996, the FIA dictated much higher cockpit rails to protect the driver. Other differences are that Formula One cars have narrower, more cramped cockpits because the car's profile is thinner. Also, Indycar drivers have fewer data screen readouts than Formula One, due to fewer onboard sensors.

Nose and rear wings

Both Formula One and Indycar organizers have different rules about the size and shape of the wings. Generally, Indycar wings are smaller and produce less downforce, due to a concern for safety. Indycars run some races on high-speed oval tracks, where speeds of over 230 mph are common. If wings were allowed to be any significant size, speeds would keep creeping up, putting drivers' lives at risk in the event of a crash. Most Formula One racing, on the other hand, is done on flat road circuits, where speeds rarely reach above 200 mph. Wings here are used for providing downforce for better handling in turns. The FIA has implemented front wing rule changes in 1996 to limit downforce thus slightly reducing speeds.

Formula One

Although there are as many as two dozen Formula One teams (the number fluctuates as some of the shoestring teams fall by the wayside when their coffers run dry), the great modern battles for victories occur between just four or five teams. Here are the teams that are generally acknowledged to be at the top of the Formula One ladder:

A 1990s contender

The Benetton team, spurred by team manager Flavio Briatore, has been one of the top teams of the 1990s, going head-to-head most often with the Williams team.

Williams and Benetton

Williams cars, primarily sponsored by Rothmans Tobacco, have won seven Formula One Constructor's Cup titles since the team, formed by Frank Williams, first started in Formula One in 1973. One of its great drivers was Nigel Mansell, who won the 1992 driver's title in a Williams FW14B with active suspension. Damon Hill, son of the late Graham Hill, is the team's current primary driver, while the number two driver is Indycar champion Jacques Villeneuve, son of the late Giles Villeneuve.

In the 1990s Williams' main competitor has been the Benetton team, which is owned by the same company that sells the colorful range of sports clothes worldwide. Running the Benetton team is Flavio Briatore, who joined them in 1989, three years after the team was formed. Although Briatore is an acknowledged genius in fielding a race car team, Benetton struggled until the arrival of driver Michael Schumacher in 1991. By 1993, the Benetton cars were beginning to equal the Williams cars, and Schumacher was a regular front-runner. In 1995, it all came together for Benetton, Schumacher beating arch-rival Damon Hill to the driving title by just one point, owing in part to many crashes that left the pair bitter enemies.

Details, details

The Williams team, owned by the legendary Frank Williams, has muscled its way to the top through meticulous engineering and attention to details.

MAKE: 1996 BENETTON B196

Construction: Carbon fiber
Length: 4125mm
Wheelbase: 2870mm
Front Track: 1670mm
Rear Track: 1600mm
Weight: 600kg (all fluids, including driver)
Tires: Goodyear Eagle radials
Brakes: Carbon-fiber discs and pads
Gearbox: Benetton seven-speed semi-automatic
Engine: Renault V10 RS8
Displacement: 3000cc
Horsepower: 800 (est.)

MAKE: 1996 WILLIAMS FW18

Construction: Carbon Aramid epoxy compound
Length: 4150mm
Front Track: 1670mm
Rear Track: 1600mm
Wheelbase: 2890mm
Weight: 600kg (all fluids, including driver)
Tires: Goodyear Eagle radials
Brakes: Carbone Industrie discs and pads. AP
calipers
Gearbox: Six-speed Williams transverse semi-
automatic
Engine: Renault V10 RS8
Displacement: 3000cc
Horsepower: 800 (est.)

Champion driver
Michael Schumacher helped Benetton make a quantum leap
forward with his masterful driving, capturing the 1995 driver's
championship.

Belgian battle
A Williams, with Damon Hill at the wheel, leads the race at Spa
during the Belgian Grand Prix in 1995.

Ferrari and McLaren

Two teams that have struggled in the 1990s, after spectacular histories, are McLaren and Ferrari. In the past, both teams have been able to lay claim to being monumental successes.

Ferrari is the name most associated with Formula One, the team having won eight Constructor's Cup titles. Enzo Ferrari put his first Formula One car on the track in 1950; since then, his cars and drivers have enjoyed a phenomenal following among racing fans. But with Enzo's death in 1988, and the company's takeover by Fiat, success has eluded Ferrari, although this has not dampened their fans' enthusiasm. The last Constructor's Cup title won by the team was in 1983, but of late their fortunes have been looking up. New engines and chassis designs have made the cars competitive again, and the hiring of Michael Schumacher to drive in 1996 could be the move that will bring glory once more to the red machines from Modena.

McLaren's fall onto hard times has been more recent. In the 1980s, in partnership with Honda and with the great Ayrton Senna at the wheel, McLaren was unbeatable. From 1984 to 1991, they won six Constructor's Cup titles, the red-and-white Marlboro-sponsored machines often finishing one-two, far ahead of the competition. Ron Dennis, the team manager, was the driving force behind this success. However, with the departure of Honda – which was eventually replaced by Mercedes-Benz – and the defection of Senna to Williams, McLaren has struggled to regain its former glory.

No match

A 1995 McLaren at speed. Despite hiring Nigel Mansell at the start of the season, the McLaren team was no match for Williams or Benetton.

Former glory

After a decade of not being contenders for the championship, in 1995 Ferrari began to show signs that their former glory might soon return.

First and second

McLaren at their peak; the late Ayrton Senna and teammate Gerhard Berger run 1-2 at Monaco.

Squabbles

The death of Enzo Ferrari in 1988 led to a number of squabbles among members of the Formula One team. The development of a new V-12 engine should help make the cars competitive again.

MAKE: 1996 McCLAREN MP4/11

Construction: Hercules Aerospace carbon fiber honeycomb composite
Length: 4145mm
Wheelbase: 2880mm
Front Track: 1675mm
Rear Track: 1605mm
Weight: 600kg (all fluids, plus driver)
Tires: Goodyear Eagle radials
Brakes: AP calipers, carbon fiber pads, discs
Gearbox: McLaren longitudinal six-speed semi-automatic
Engine: Mercedes-Benz F0110 V-10
Displacement: 3000cc
Horsepower: 800 (est.)

MAKE: 1996 FERRARI F310

Construction: Carbon-fiber and honeycomb composite
Length: 4355mm
Wheelbase: 2900mm
Front Track: 1690mm
Rear Track: 1605mm
Weight: 600kg (all fluids, including driver)
Tires: Goodyear Eagle radials
Brakes: Ventilated carbon discs
Gearbox: Six-speed Ferrari semi-automatic
Engine: Ferrari 046
Displacement: 2998.1cc
Horsepower: 800 (est.)

Indycar

Penske and Lola

In the past 10 years, the two dominant chassis makers on the Indycar circuit have been Penske and Lola. In the main, the former's banner has been carried by Emerson Fittipaldi, Al Unser Jr, and Rick Mears, while Michael Andretti, Mario Andretti and, for one season, Formula One champion Nigel Mansell have done the honors for the latter. Other teams also use the Lola chassis, such as the Jim Hall Pennzoil team with driver Gil de Feran.

The Penske chassis is built in England by a subsidiary of Roger Penske's racing organization. Penske, who fielded a Formula One team in the late 1970s, is one of the great businessmen of racing. He has amassed an amazing 10 wins for his team at the Indianapolis Motor Speedway.

The Lola chassis is also built in England, its distributor in the United States being Carl Haas of Chicago, whose team is the primary development group for the chassis.

Haas, whose partner is film star Paul Newman, has won several Indycar championships in the past 10 years, thanks to Michael Andretti and his father, Mario. But a win at the Indianapolis 500 has eluded his team, although a number of other teams using Lola chassis have been in the victory circle at Indianapolis and elsewhere.

MAKE: 1996 PENSKE PC25

Construction: Penske carbon fiber
Length: 190 inches
Wheelbase: 115 inches
Front Track: 68 inches
Rear Track: 64 inches
Weight: 1,550 pounds (all fluids, minus driver)
Tires: Goodyear Eagle radials
Brakes: Alcon cast-iron discs with carbon-fiber pads
Gearbox: Six-speed manual
Engine: Mercedes-Benz Ilmor IC 108
Displacement: 2.65 liters
Horsepower: 800 @ 13,000 rpm

Lola chassis
The Jim Hall/Pennzoil team, with Brazilian Gil de Feran driving, uses the Lola chassis.

Bobby Rahal, a two-time Indianapolis champion, pilots his Mercedes-powered Lola through a turn.

MAKE: 1996 LOLA T96/00

Construction: Carbon fiber
Length: 192 inches
Wheelbase: 118 inches
Front Track: 69 inches
Rear Track: 64 inches
Weight: 1,550 pounds (all fluids, minus driver)
Tires: Varies by team: either Goodyear Eagle or Firestone Firehawk
Brakes: Brembo cast-iron discs with carbon-fiber pads
Gearbox: Lola transverse six-speed manual
Engine: Varies by team: either Ford-Cosworth, Honda or Mercedes-Benz
Displacement: 2.65 liters
Horsepower: 800 (est.)

Andretti at speed
The chief team effort for Lola has been the Newman-Haas team, which has as its chief driver Michael Andretti. In past years, the team has seen wins with Nigel mansell and Mario Andretti.

Early test
Without its sponsors' markings, a Mercedes-powered Penske receives an early-season test at the Homestead Motorsports Park near Miami, Fla.

Toyota and Reynard

Two chassis that are newcomers to the Indycar fray are the Reynard, which is fast challenging Lola as the most widely used chassis, and the Dan Gurney AAR chassis used by the fledgling Toyota team. Although both designs are similar, the Gurney effort is an all-American chassis built in California.

So far, Reynard has enjoyed greater success, having won the 1995 Indianapolis 500 and the 1995 championship for Team Green with Jacques Villeneuve at the wheel. In 1996, as many as a dozen teams were using the Reynard chassis, with Lola and Penske being the next favorite choices.

The Gurney AAR chassis still has a long way to go. At the first race of the 1996 season in Miami, with Juan Manuel Fangio II at the controls, the Toyota qualified last and never looked competitive. Whether that was due to a lack of power from the Toyota V-8, or handling and aerodynamic problems with the chassis remains to be seen.

MAKE: 1996 TOYOTA AAR EAGLE MKV

Construction: Carbon fiber
Length: 195 inches
Wheelbase: 117 inches
Front Track: 67 inches
Rear Track: 63 inches
Weight: 1,550 pounds (all fluids, minus driver)
Tires: Goodyear Eagles
Brakes: AP cast-iron discs with carbon-fiber pads
Gearbox: Xtrac six-speed manual
Engine: Toyota RV8A
Displacement: 2.65 liters
Horsepower: 750 (est.)

MAKE: 1996 REYNARD 961

Construction: Carbon fiber
Length: 4970mm
Wheelbase: 3050mm
Front Track: 1720mm
Rear Track: 1620mm
Weight: 1,550 pounds (all fluids, minus driver)
Tires: Varies by team: either Goodyear Eagle or Firestone Firehawk
Brakes: Brembo cast-iron discs with carbon-fiber pads
Gearbox: Xtrac six-speed manual
Engine: Varies by team: either Ford-Cosworth, Honda or Mercedes-Benz
Displacement: 2.65 liters
Horsepower: 800 (est.)

Indy winner

Jacques Villeneuve, driving for Team Green in 1995, took the Ford-powered Reynard to a win at Indianapolis and picked up the season championship.

Toyota power

The newest manufacturer to enter the Indycar war is Toyota, which began supplying engines to two teams in 1998. This is the Areiero/Wells entry with rookie Jeff Krosnoff at the wheel.

Factory team

The chief Toyota effort is being led by Dan Gurney's All-American Racers. Using a Gurney-designed Eagle chassis, the AAR team has done all of the development work on the Toyota, with Juan Manuel Fangio II as the driver.

Computers and Racing

In all forms of racing, the person with the degree in computer engineering and electronics has replaced the simple mechanic as the team member who makes the car go fast. It wasn't so long ago that race fans and performance car enthusiasts decried the use of computer controls on passenger car engines as a means of cleaning up exhaust pollution. All those wires and mysterious black boxes couldn't replace a good old carburetor, big pistons, and a hot camshaft. They couldn't have been more wrong.

Power on tap

Thanks to the use of sophisticated engine management computers, the Peugeot engine in this Formula One car can develop as much as 800 horsepower from a 3-liter design.

Computing power equals horsepower

Today, performance street cars are faster and more reliable as a direct result of onboard computers that monitor dozens of engine and transmission functions. The same evolution has occurred in virtually every aspect of racing. Computing power has become almost as important as horsepower. More correctly, in a modern race car, you can't have one without the other.

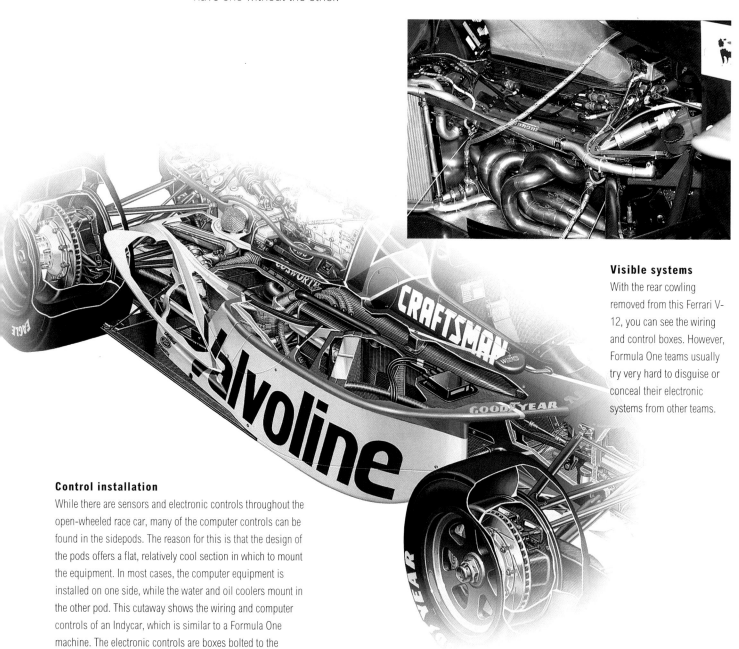

Visible systems
With the rear cowling removed from this Ferrari V-12, you can see the wiring and control boxes. However, Formula One teams usually try very hard to disguise or conceal their electronic systems from other teams.

Control installation
While there are sensors and electronic controls throughout the open-wheeled race car, many of the computer controls can be found in the sidepods. The reason for this is that the design of the pods offers a flat, relatively cool section in which to mount the equipment. In most cases, the computer equipment is installed on one side, while the water and oil coolers mount in the other pod. This cutaway shows the wiring and computer controls of an Indycar, which is similar to a Formula One machine. The electronic controls are boxes bolted to the sidepod floor. They consist of a small battery, an ECU (electronic control unit), a spark control box, an alternator control box, and a control unit that sends data to the driver's digital cockpit screen.

Checking the data
When a driver pulls into the pits after a few test laps, engineers armed with laptop computers and other monitoring devices grab vital data from the on-board systems to check engine performance.

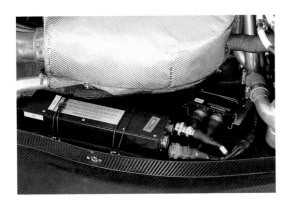

Electronic control unit
Here is a close-up of the battery (slim, rectangular box) and the electronic control unit of a Ford-powered Reynard. The ECU takes all the readings from the separate engine systems – the fuel delivery and the air intake or turbocharger – and sends it to the spark control box (which, in this case, is mounted closer to the engine). This adjusts the timing of the firing of the spark plugs.

Concealed functions
As with the Ferrari, the electronics of this Tyrrell are also visible, although their exact functions are not revealed. Because of concerns by the FIA about illegal active suspension setups, they routinely monitor the software in the teams' cars to make sure that there are no hidden surprises.

The cockpit

Imagine trying to read a computer at 200 mph, because that's exactly what a Formula One driver has to do. In addition to the normal hand and foot controls, the cockpit of a Formula One race car features an array of liquid crystal diode computer screens that keep the driver informed about his car's performance. Information displayed includes the engine's rpm, which is shown on the center screen, usually in a band that runs from left to right. Also on that screen will be some indication of the gear selected and a fuel pressure indicator. Auxiliary screens will show the engine coolant temperature, oil temperature and pressure, and lap times. Some very sophisticated setups allow the pit crew to send messages that appear on the screen, such as where the driver is running in the field and when he should come in for a pit stop.

Computer screens
This shot of the cockpit of a Formula One car shows the three computer screens that provide the driver with all the information he needs about his car and his race performance. Note the button on the steering wheel labeled "scroll." It allows the driver to change the displays to the information he is seeking. The other buttons on the wheel activate the two-way radio, and can reset the fuel pressure and lap times. The gear shift is not visible in this view, but is a paddle just behind the wheel. Flick it back and the semi-automatic gearbox shifts up a gear; flick it forward and it shifts down.

Lap times

Damon Hill sits in the cockpit of his Williams-Renault watching a computer screen that displays the lap times of other drivers on the course during practice, as well as his own previous lap times.

Essential information

In this car's cockpit, there is just one information display. Some drivers prefer a display that gives them only the essentials – rpm, gear selection, fuel pressure, oil and coolant temperature, and oil pressure. Note that the steering wheel has been removed from its shaft. All race cars have removable wheels so that the driver can squeeze down into the seat.

Analog gauges

So what would a cockpit be like without all the electronic equipment? Something like this 1996 NASCAR stock car. Note the single row of round, analog gauges, with the tachometer in the center. The only concession to 1990s technology is the two-way radio, which is activated by a button on the steering wheel.

High tech versus low tech

Aside from communications, computers in the race car control virtually every function short of actually pressing the gas pedal or the brake. They monitor engine combustion, air intake, fuel flow, chassis and shock absorber movement, and transmission shift points. Incredibly, the computers of a modern Formula One race car are many times more powerful than the computers that took US astronauts to the moon in 1969.

Without proper computer work and electronic functions – from engine performance and chassis setup to communications – it would be impossible for a race team to even qualify for an event.

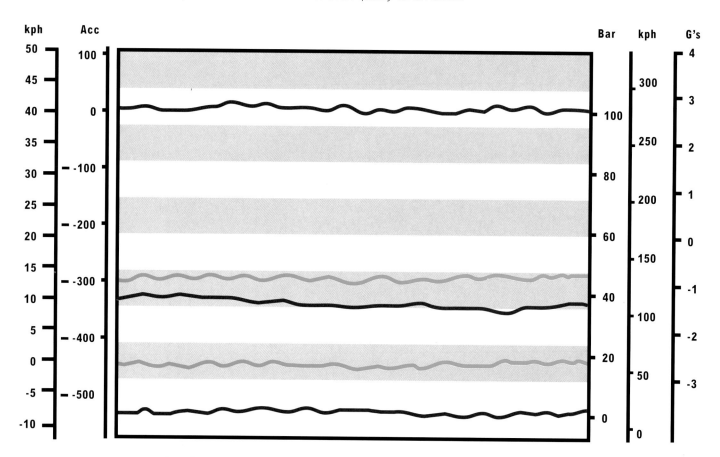

Accelerometers

Despite the lack of electronic controls in the engine bay, NASCAR teams do use telemetry during testing to help set up the car. Accelerometers are used on the chassis to measure movement through the turns, and that data helps the engineers tune the chassis for each race. According to NASCAR rules, however, all of those sensors and transmitters must be removed from the car before qualifying and the race itself.

Data transmission

All the data gathered by the ECM is sent to this telemetry control module that transmits the information to the engineers in the pits, or stores it until the engineer plugs his laptop computer into the module and downloads it.

Electronic controls

In two of the most popular forms of auto racing, you can see the extremes of technology. On this Ford Cosworth XD Indycar engine, you can see the electronic control module (ECM) and all the leads that run from it to the engine and other control boxes. The ECM makes all the decisions for the engine, and it allows engineers to squeeze upward of 650 horsepower from a V-8 with a capacity of just 2.65 liters.

Pit control

When Jackie Stewart won his Formula One championships in the 1970s, the primary means of communication between driver and crew was the pit board. Often, this was a simple chalk board on which a crew member scrawled information about the driver's position, how far behind (or ahead) he was, and when he should come in for fuel. Really fancy teams had dayglo orange plastic letters and numbers that clipped to a panel. This information was waved at the driver when he went by at 160 mph or more. A wave of his hand meant that he understood the message.

Today, a driver has a radio set in his helmet and can communicate instantly with his pit crew from any spot on the race track.

Often, the crew knows more than the driver, because an array of sensors is continuously transmitting data on the car's performance to the computers in the pit, telling the crew where the driver is fast or where he needs to pick up speed. The sensors also download masses of information about engine condition, fuel mileage, transmission functions, and other critical factors.

Car sensors

Sensors in the car are transmitting data about the cars performance continuously so the crew know exactly what is happening on the race track.

Monitors

Like Mission Control at the Kennedy Space Center, no modern Formula One pit would be complete without a bank of monitors to keep the team manager informed of what is happening on the track. This setup for Team Benetton, which runs a two-car team, is fairly typical of what is needed to keep up with the action. The monitors provide continuous real-time updates of telemetry from the race cars; the feed from the official timing and scoring officials, which shows the positions of all the cars on the track; and a satellite feed of the television broadcast of the race so that they can see action around the track. The last is vitally important because the crew has a very limited view of the action from the inside of the pits.

Driver's value

No matter how useful the pit lane telemetry, an engineer's best source of data is still the driver. Here, a Cosworth engineer and Indycar driver Raul Boesel discuss how the engine is performing at high rpm on an oval track.

Engine data

During practice, Ford Cosworth engineers keep track of the performance of their engine while the car is on the track. The data on the screen shows the engine rpm at various throttle positions, as well as cylinder temperatures, and information on spark advance and the flow of exhaust gases.

Aerodynamics

If there is one reason why most race cars are faster today than they have ever been, it's the advent of aerodynamics. Those wings on the front and back, those wide sidepods, even the shape of the driver's helmet, all contribute to making a car faster. In this chapter we'll examine how the various aero aids do their job of effectively knifing through the air, and how a tweak here or a twist there can mean the difference between running at the front and bringing up the rear.

Using the wind

With top speeds in excess of 200 mph at many tracks around the world, the aerodynamics aids are the items that keep a race car on the track.

Airflow

At one time, race teams focused almost solely on developing engine power, for obvious reasons. More horsepower meant higher speeds. And if you had more horsepower than the other fellow on the starting grid, you were almost assured of victory – provided nothing broke.

After a while, however, any increases in the horsepower available from engines that were restricted to a certain displacement by the race rules were minimal. The difference in power between the engines of one team and another were often only 50 horses or less.

So race car designers began looking at aerodynamics as a means of increasing speed. It seemed a simple discovery – reduce the air resistance that the engine had to overcome to move the race car, and you could go faster with no increase in horsepower. But nothing is simple when you're in 200 mph territory.

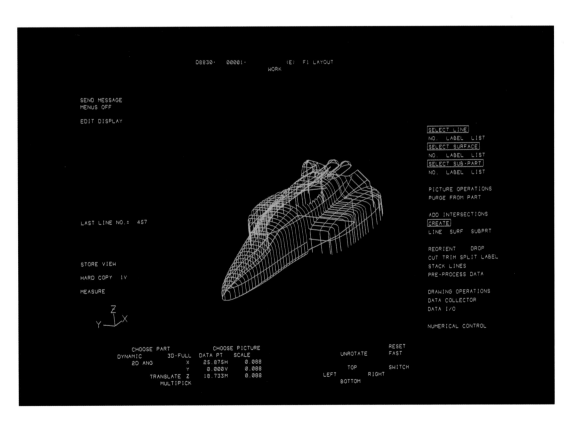

Sophisticated programs

When designing the chassis of a modern Formula One racer or Indycar, engineers use sophisticated computer programs that allow them to view the proposed shape – in this case, the nose and cockpit cowl – from all angles. The computer can assess the overall aerodynamic performance, and a few keystrokes allow an engineer to quickly decide if a proposed change improves or diminishes the design. Although such work is highly technical, and the equipment needed to accomplish it very expensive, this is a vast improvement over the days when race teams actually had to build an entire car, then test it to see if it worked. If it failed, it was literally a case of having to go back to the drawing board.

Test-bed

A prototype is put on a test-bed, where it is run through a variety of procedures, including a check for wind resistance. The test-bed and the chassis are wired with a variety of sensors that are linked to a computer, which records every minute change that the engineers make. With such exact baselines, engineers can accurately determine the effect even the smallest of changes will have in the race car's overall performance on the track.

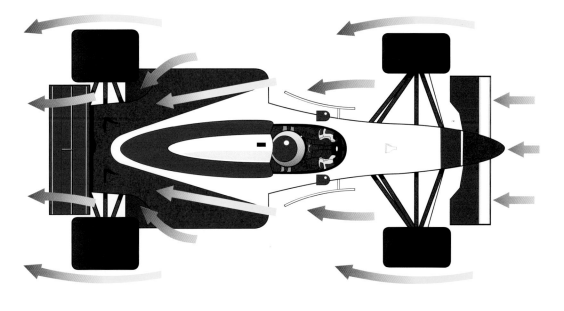

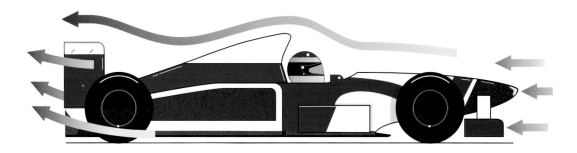

Splitting the wind

The aerodynamic package of a modern formula race car is designed to split the wind. The majority of the airflow passes up and over the car, pushing down on the front wings, then sweeping over the cockpit and into the rear wing, where it applies additional downforce. The front wing also deflects air straight back into the sidepods, where the oil and coolant radiators reside. The air that flows into the sidepods is also ejected upward into the rear wing to help create downforce.

Viewed from above, the air is directed around the nose and tires, into and over the sidepods, and up and over the rear wing.

Wings

Until the 1980s, the science of aerodynamics was applied almost haphazardly by most race teams. Shapes were tried because they looked sleek; wings large and small were attached at front and back during track testing. Sometimes everything worked, but at others it was a disaster. This "seat-of-your-pants" engineering continued until some of the more sophisticated Formula One and Indycar teams began to employ aerospace wind tunnels and computer simulations in an attempt to achieve perfect race car aerodynamics.

The results were astounding.

Aerodynamic drag
The late Ayrton Senna grabs the apex of a turn. What teams like McLaren have learned is that overall lap times come down with effective use of wings, although overall top speed on the straights may be lower because of aerodynamic drag.

Early developments

This 1970 Lotus 72C shows some early developments in front and rear wings. One of the first lessons learned about rear wings was to mount them directly to the chassis, rather than to the suspension. Such a setup greatly increased the direct force on the rear wheels.

Increased grip

The added downforce of the wings makes it possible for cars to move more quickly around turns, because it increases the grip of the front tires. Wings can be tuned to create or eliminate understeer and oversteer.

Current practice

Mika Hakkinen's 1995 McLaren shows the current theory on wings. Note the small third wing behind the driver's cockpit.

Wickerbills

The 200 mph speeds seen in Formula One and Indycar are made possible by aerodynamics that were developed scientifically; today's race cars are very efficient at dealing with airflow when they first roll out of the shop. Teams work within a very narrow range of changes to hone the entire aerodynamic package.

Auto racing has become a game of inches – or more correctly, a game of millimeters and degrees. A key to tuning the front wing is the manner in which the air comes off the trailing edge. Rather than being reshaped for different conditions, the wing is built with a removable "wickerbill." This thin strip of aluminum is used to make a small adjustment in the angle of the wing.

Side plate

At each end of the wing is a side plate, which serves several functions. It helps channel air into the front wing and around the front wheels and tires, which can create tremendous drag that will slow a car. The length of the side plate also affects the airflow back to the sidepods. The longer the side plate, the more cleanly air flows to the rear.

Adjustments

A mechanic can slide out one wickerbill and replace it with another that either increases or decreases the angle of the wing by as little as a half-degree. Another adjustment to the overall angle of the front wing can be made during a race by turning a small key at the side of the wing. One twist is equal to a half-degree. If the angle of the wing was changed by a full degree, it would dramatically alter the car's handling.

GURNEY AND THE "GURNEY FLAP"

As a race car driver and, later, a team owner, Dan Gurney has always been at the forefront of race car development. In the 1960s, Gurney was a winning driver and campaigned his Eagle race cars in Formula One.

In the 1970s, his all-American Eagle Indycars were winners at the Indianapolis 500, dominating the venue for many years.

Today, he is the driving force behind Toyota's fledgling effort to break into the Indycar ranks. Their engines are combined with Gurney's latest All-American Racers chassis, which are designed and built in the United States.

On Indycars there is a little bit of Dan Gurney ingenuity that first appeared on Gurney's Indycars in the 1970s. Called a wickerbill by some, the small, adjustable lip found on the back of the rear wings of Indycars is known to racers as a "Gurney Flap."

Dan Gurney first used these metal lips on the edges of his cars' wings at Indianapolis as a way of increasing the efficiency of the large rear wings at high speeds. Acting much like the flaps on an airplane wing, the Gurney Flap helps clean up the airflow as it comes off the rear wing, maintaining maximum downforce. The little aero aid has proven its effectiveness over more than two decades of use, and the man's name who first tried it on a race car has also stuck.

Down on power
On this Ferrari, the front wing is relatively small when compared to the rear wing. This is a tradeoff that will produce higher top speeds, but slower cornering speeds, perhaps indicating that the Ferrari's V-12 was down on power.

Rear aerodynamics

Like the front wing, the rear wing of a race car also has many elements, among them a wickerbill at the trailing edge. Because of the wing's increased size in relationship to the front wing, and the higher angle of attack, the rear wickerbill is even more critical to the car's handling.

Low angle of attack

High angle of attack

Separated flow

High angle with wickerbill

Smoothing airflow

This diagram shows what happens to the air as it sweeps over a wing. Without a wickerbill, the air passing over the underside of the wing tends to pull away from it, actually reducing downforce. The wickerbill acts like a flap on an airplane, smoothing out the airflow so that sustained downforce is maintained.

Constant change

Like front wings, the rear airfoils on Formula One cars are constantly under change as teams look for any possible advantage. This shot of a Williams in testing at Estoril, Portugal, shows that there are actually two airfoils to the rear wing, the lower plane being mounted in a V-shape, perhaps to take advantage of the way in which the air sweeps off the lower bodywork.

Oval use

This wickerbill is on a 1995 Reynard set up for a high-speed oval.

Third wing

McLaren was the lone competitor in 1995 to add a third wing to its cars, a small airfoil being mounted just behind the driver's cockpit. The team had a less-than-successful year in 1995, so there is no way of knowing if the wing was an advantage. Its small size suggests that its main purpose is to improve airflow to the rear wing, rather than provide any significant downforce.

Creating lift

Even if a car doesn't fly off the track, ill-adjusted wings can result in lift, where enough air pressure builds up beneath a front wing to literally lift the front end off the ground. This can be made worse by a bump in the track.

Downforce

Creating an aerodynamic race car design is not a simple matter. There are trade-offs.

A design that cuts through the air with very little resistance will be fast in a straight line, but offer almost no help when braking and negotiating a turn. On the other hand, a design that helps keep a car glued to the track in the turns can be too slow on the straightaways. So a race car designer must seek a strategic compromise.

For the most part, the compromise involves drag and downforce. Drag, expressed as a percentage, is how much air resistance a car encounters. Downforce, measured in pounds per square inch, is how firmly the car is pressed to the track. There's a third factor called lift, which is the opposite of downforce and must be avoided.

Inverted airfoil

Like the Wright brothers when they were designing early airplanes, race teams start with the basic shape of an airfoil. On a plane, the airfoil is designed so that the air produces greater pressure on the underside of the wing to create lift. On a race car, the exact opposite is the goal. The airfoil is inverted so that the air creates pressure on top of the wing and presses downward, increasing the grip of the tires. That's called downforce. Set the wing angle too steeply, and it generates too much downforce and increases the drag coefficient. The higher the drag coefficient, the more horsepower that is needed to push the car.

WING CONFIGURATIONS

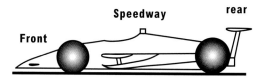

Speedway

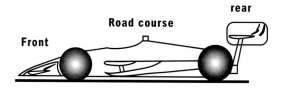

Road course

Wide body

Downforce can be created by features other than wings. This wide body is shaped in such a way as to act like an airfoil, although it is very crude by modern standards. In practice, it probably did as much to create unwanted drag as it did to create downforce.

No help

When a car gets bumped at the start and goes airborne, the aerodynamic package is of little use. Keep it on the ground, however, and the aerodynamics of a Formula One car will greatly enhance its performance.

Flat shape

On this 1970s Ferrari, the flat front wing is an attempt to create a shape that will not inhibit straight-line speed, but will provide some downforce in the turns and under braking.

Ground effects

As teams such as Lotus explored what happened to race cars when large rear wings were employed, they discovered a great offshoot of aerodynamics called "ground effects." This made use of the low pressure created beneath the car, by the air sweeping over and under it, to literally suck the chassis to the pavement. This improved cornering abilities tremendously.

Ducts and skirts

One of the cars that most effectively used ground effects was this Lotus Type 88. A series of ducts and flexible side skirts was used to sweep the air from under the car and create a vacuum. The faster the car went, the greater the vacuum, and the more it hugged the road. The Lotus Type 88 was revolutionary and unbeatable. The only drawback was that if the suction was broken – if the car hit a bump, for example – the driver could abruptly lose control.

Fan assistance

Having caught on to the ground effects game, Brabham took it a step further. They mounted two electrically-powered fans at the back of the car to suck any air from beneath it and create even more vacuum. So effective was the system that the car won first time out, but then it was banned from Formula One competition.

The basics

When Formula One cars first began experimenting with wings, the attention was at the rear, to improve braking and cornering in turns by increasing the downforce on the rear wheels. This Lotus used a huge rear wing, but no aids at the front.

Ride height

Although extreme ground effects are banned on today's Formula One racers and Indycars, engineers still manage to create some ground effects by keeping ride height low and directing as much air as possible from under the car. The ride height is determined by the geometry of the coil springs and the pushrods attached to the bellcranks on the dampers. The lower the ride height, the less air that gets under the car. In recent years, Formula One and Indycar officials have limited the amount of vacuum that can be generated by setting ride height limits and enforcing them by requiring a wooden skid pad to be fitted to the bottom of the car. If the pad wears more than a specified amount in a race (because the ride height is too low), the car will be disqualified.

Other Aero Aids

Aside from wings and sidepods, modern race cars use a variety of other small aero aids to improve airflow. Most common are diffusers or vortex generators, which help direct the flow of air in such a way as to enhance downforce, but reduce drag by smoothing the turbulence of the air that comes off other parts of the car.

Downforce
Diffusers in front of the sidepods and a flat bottom on this Benetton create downforce, much like the ground effects cars.

Reducing turbulence
This panel at the front of the sidepod of a 1996 Reynard is intended to reduce turbulence produced by the front wing and wheels.

Helmet help
Even the driver's helmet becomes an aero aid. This is Raul Boesel's helmet; notice the ripples on top that help direct air past the cockpit.

Sweeping air
This pod at the back of the Reynard's sidepod helps sweep air up and over the spinning rear tires, which create their own drag.

Turbulent exhaust
The hot exhaust gases created by the engine are also managed as a part of the airflow package. The turbocharger on this Indycar discharges turbulent exhaust that must be directed in such a way as to enhance, not upset, the aerodynamics.

Historical designs

Since, in Formula One, teams are relatively free to try whatever innovation they think will result in a faster car, some interesting designs have been seen over the years.

Six wheels

Among the most bizarre designs was the six-wheel Project 34 Tyrrell, which raced and won an event in 1976. The theory was that four small front wheels would put more rubber on the road, yet present less aerodynamic drag at the front than two, taller wheels. After a brief moment of glory, the design proved unworkable and it was retired.

Side plate design
On this car, driven by Niki Lauda, the front wing was designed with the side plates in the downward position. Today, the theory is exactly the opposite.

Initial thinking
In the late 1970s, this McLaren, driven by Britain's James Hunt, showed the initial thinking about advanced aerodynamics: make the car wide like a wing to cut through the air. Research would later show that narrow, low-profile designs were better.

Wide body
As the use of aerodynamics became more sophisticated, teams widened the body panels to give them more surface to work with to direct the flow of air over the vehicle. However, the wide bodies presented their own problem with drag that limited top speeds.

Aerodynamic experiments

In Formula One, there are conflicting theories about the best height for front wings, showing that a lot of aerodynamic experimentation is still going on. Wing sizes have also varied. Although the FIA sets a maximum size, there is no minimum size, and at certain tracks some teams find that a smaller wing works better.

During practice, the setting of the wings, both front and back, is one area to which teams pay particular attention. They will experiment with various angles, and sometimes the settings can cause the car's handling to go awry, as it likely did with this Williams.

When track conditions get wet, teams will experiment with greater downforce. The higher wing setting will limit straight-line speed, but in the slippery turns will result in better grip. Because Formula One cars frequently run in the rain, teams spend a lot of time working on wet settings.

Altered size

Over the years, race teams have tried altering the sizes of the wings. In some cases, a smaller wing has proved more effective than a large one.

Following suit

The Williams front wing arrangement proved so effective that toward the end of the 1995 season, other teams began to experiment with similar designs.

High wing

Williams has gone to a higher front wing. This is set at an angle in an effort to maintain downforce, but reduce some of the drag.

New rules

About every five years or so, it seems like the engineers have reached a point where rules makers become concerned about the speeds the cars are attaining. While paramount concern is for driver safety, the rules makers, whether it is in Indycars or Formula One, also are concerned to a degree for team parity and cost containment. So when they sense that something is getting out of hand, they jump in and change the basic ground rules. The most recent changes have had to do with reducing the amount of downforce generated by the cars in turns, as well as new regulations to protect the driver's cockpit in the event of a crash.

Less grip

Damon Hill hits the brakes at the entrance to a turn, an area where downforce has a great effect. For 1996, the FIA – sanctioning body for Formula One – mandated new, higher minimum ride heights as a way of cutting back on downforce and lowering speeds in corners, which is where most severe crashes occur.

Better protection

Another change to the rules was the stipulation that the sides of the cockpit had to come up higher to protect the driver from objects, such as tires, flying into the cockpit. Some teams used a design that not only protected the driver but enhanced air flow.

RECENT RULES CHANGES

There was once a time when the top two forms of auto racing – Formula One and Indycar – were venues where the quest was for all-out speed and performance. But starting in the mid 1980s, technology was pushing the speeds into dangerous territory.

Racing has always been a dangerous and sometimes lethal sport, but as top speeds routinely began to stay above 200 mph, organizers and some race teams began to worry about the ability to build cars that would keep the drivers alive in all but the most catastrophic crashes.

Starting in the 1980s, the series organizing bodies began to alter the rules to rein in the speeds – and some of the astronomical costs – as well as stipulate to uniform cockpit safety measures. Although there have continued to be deaths in racing – most notably the passing of Ayrton Senna in 1994 – there is no argument that race cars today are safer than ever before.

And even though a number of rules have been enacted to help keep speeds from progressing as rapidly as they once were, engineers are still finding ways to squeeze a little more speed from the cars within the rules.

In 1995 and 1996, both Formula One and Indycars were put under a new round of safety and aerodynamic changes. Here is a rundown on the latest rules changes:

Formula One

Aerodynamics:
Starting with the 1995 season, the FIA – sanctioning body of Formula One – continued its effort to lower the amount of downforce that cars could generate by raising the minimum ground clearance, setting smaller maximum wing sizes, and limiting the amount that any bodywork can hang out beyond the front or rear wheels. The effect of these changes was to take away as much as 30 percent of the downforce that cars were generating on the fastest circuits before the rules changes.

Engine:
The biggest change came after 1994 when the 3.5-liter engines were banned in favor of smaller 3-liter engines. While the horsepower difference between the larger and smaller engines was at first as much as 100 horsepower, by the start of the 1996 season most observers believed that the gap had been closed through technology to 50 horsepower or less. Rules also limit the size and placement of the fresh air ducting to the engine so as to eliminate an effort by some teams to create a vortex chamber that would act somewhat like a supercharger.

Weight:
The minimum weight was raised to 600kg from 505kg in 1994. But the change was largely cosmetic because the new weight includes the driver.

Cockpit:
Here is where the greatest changes can be seen by a spectator. Starting in 1995 and continuing into 1996, the FIA began a series of changes that should significantly improve driver safety. An area called the survival cell must envelop the driver from just behind his head to a point 300mm in front of his feet, which cannot extent beyond the front axle line. Also, new, higher side panels were ordered as a way of better protecting the driver's head in a crash. New regulations also covered a mandatory head rest and the maximum opening of the cockpit itself.

Aerodynamic limits
Changes to the Indycar rules involved greater limits on the aerodynamic package, including the ride height and placement of the front wings.

Small but significant changes
At speed, this 1996 Team Green Reynard appears to be largely unchanged from the previous year. But downforce on the faster ovals was reduced by as much as 30 percent by the new rules changes.

Cutting top speeds
For the Indycars, many of the rules changes were designed to limit top speeds at the faster ovals, such as the Homestead Motorsports Complex in Miami, Fla.

Race setups

Mainly as a result of improved aerodynamics, qualifying times at the Indianapolis 500 have rocketed upward. In 1962, Parnelli Jones cracked the 150 mph barrier. It took another 16 years before 200 mph was topped by Tom Sneva in 1978. This was more or less the benchmark until 1984, when speeds started to take off again. By 1992, the qualifying record at Indy was over 233 mph, but the horsepower output was not much more than it had been in Parnelli Jones' day.

Road course

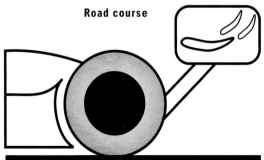

Slow-speed cornering
Set properly, the wings on a race car can generate enough downforce to improve cornering even at slow speeds. However, aerodynamics become less important than other handling factors as speed decreases.

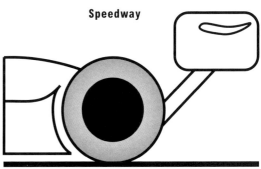

Speedway

Tremendous downforce

On the big speedways, there is generally no braking going into the turns, and the throttle is open all the way around. The wings generate tremendous downforce – as much as 3,200 pounds over the entire car – to help keep the car glued to the corners. Such downforce means that cars can generate as much as 4g in the turns.

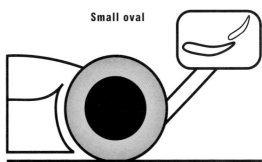

Small oval

Difficult task

Setting up a race car aerodynamically for a small oval is probably the trickiest task an Indycar team faces, because these tracks tend to have tight, banked turns and short straightaways. They are fast, but the tight turns demand a lot of downforce when the car is decelerating.

Formula One challenge

The two courses on the Formula One circuit that test the extremes of aerodynamics are Monaco and Monza. At Monaco, the course is mostly tight turns with just a few high-speed straightaways, while Italy's Monza race track, with its long straights and gentle turns, is among the fastest of the Formula One tracks.

High-speed turns
Long straightaways and turns, where very little braking is required, force Formula One teams to set the wings so that they do not generate so much downforce that they significantly decrease top speed. Instead, the aim is to push the car down enough so that it has grip for the high-speed turns.

Narrow streets
One of the major challenges at Monaco is the narrow urban streets. On parts of the track, only a retaining wall separates the cars from the harbor.

Negligible role
A McLaren leads a pack of cars through one of the hairpins at Monaco at a very slow speed. At such velocities, the wings play an almost negligible role.

Aerodynamic considerations
At other parts of the Monaco street track, such as the famed tunnel, speeds climb sharply, and the aerodynamics of the wings and sidepods must be considered.

Fast response
Moving through a chicane, the downforce to the front wheels is critical because of the quick directional changes the driver has to make while working through the turns.

No help
When a driver takes a fast way through the corner and it involves running up over the curbing, the aerodynamic grip is lost and the wings and other aero aids are of almost no use.

NASCAR aerodynamics

NASCAR stock cars present their own specialized set of aerodynamic rules and problems. Because they are closed-body cars, they present smoother aerodynamic shapes than open-wheeled cars.

Unfair advantage?
One debate that has been hot in NASCAR for several years is whether the Chevrolet Monte Carlo has an unfair aerodynamic advantage because of its roof line and nose. Dale Earnhardt has won seven championships in Chevrolets.

Aerodynamic parity
One of the stated goals of NASCAR is to keep the cars, regardless of marque, similar. One way they do that is to strictly monitor the aerodynamics of each model and set certain standards for each marque so no one car gets an advantage.

Fast and heavy
Despite their street car apearances, the NASCAR stock cars are very fast machines, capable of more than 200 mph, despite weighing more than 3,000 pounds – more than double the weight of a Formula One or Indycar.

Restrictions

The rules in NASCAR limit what teams can do to create downforce and enhance the cornering abilities of the cars which run almost exclusively on ovals. No huge rear wings are allowed, nor are large front airfoils.

Rear spoiler

The only truly active aero device on a NASCAR stock car is the rear spoiler, which is an aluminum panel riveted to the trunk lid. NASCAR rules limit the angle of this spoiler to no more than 60 degrees.

Close competition

Aerodynamics are one way that NASCAR has kept all of the cars closely competitive. Unlike Formula One, NASCAR officials aim to provide a close show for the fans. So when one type of car becomes too dominant because of its natural body shape, the rule makers start allowing the other teams to make aerodynamic tweaks that will make them faster.

Nose to tail

In NASCAR competition, the cars run so close together that drafting is a skill that drivers must learn if they are to be competitive. At tracks such as Daytona it is not unusual for drivers to link up in a 30-car draft at 200 mph.

The Kid

24-year-old Jeff Gordon became the phenom of NASCAR in 1995 when he took the championship. It's a measure of how close the competition is in NASCAR that although Gordon won the title, 16 drivers visited the winner's circle that year. Because the race cars are limited when it comes to aerodynamics and engines, some argue that driver talent matters more here than in any other series.

Barrel roll

Because of their enclosed cockpits, NASCAR stock cars are prone to lift off the ground during crashes at high speed, often causing the spectacular sight of a 3,500-pound car doing a barrel roll. One way in which NASCAR has helped reduce that danger is to allow the installation of roof flaps that lift when air pressure inside the cockpit starts to push on the roof. The flaps open, air escapes, and with luck, the car stays on the ground.

A fast pack

The jewel race in the NASCAR circuit is the Daytona 500, which starts the season in February and always features close running among more than 40 cars.

Engines and Transmissions

If you think of a modern race car as a series of components that are simply plugged into the chassis, you will better understand the role that the engine plays in just about all forms of racing today. In the past, teams often developed their own engines, or bought basic blocks from manufacturers and added their own special equipment. Not any more. With the advent of space-age technology, engine building has become a specialized art that is too expensive for any one team to develop on their own.

Looking for speed

Although the days are gone when teams built and modified their own engines, the quest for more hosepower by the engine manufacturers is an expensive and complex pursuit. This Team Green Reynard has Ford power on board.

Formula One versus Indy

Today's Formula One and Indycar teams rely on engine suppliers like Cosworth, Ilmor, Renault, Honda, Yamaha, and Toyota to provide complete engine packages, which they just plug into their chassis. Most teams have nothing to do with the engines; the suppliers send their own engineers to look after the powerplants during testing and racing. They are also contracted to supply engines for the entire season, so that when a replacement is needed it will be available.

In Formula One, the relationship between teams and engine builders is close, but engines are switched around, depending on the source of sponsorship money. McLaren is the customer of Ilmor Engineering, which supplies engines sponsored by Mercedes-Benz; Williams uses engines by Renault, and Tyrrell employs Yamaha.

In Indycar, the rules dictate that an engine supplier must support at least two teams, so it's not uncommon to find many teams running the same engine. For years it was the Ilmor-built Chevrolet V-8, then it was the Ford-Cosworth XD, and now it is the Honda V-8.

Formula One and Indy engines

Ilmor Engineering has been successful in developing winning Formula One and Indycar engines. Although much of the technology is similar in both series, there are significant differences between the engines. The two engines shown here are designs that are no longer in use, but were the basis for the engines that are being raced today. The Chevrolet Indy A engine led to the Mercedes-Benz Indy engine. The technology is Ilmor, but first Chevrolet, then Mercedes-Benz, provided sponsorship money in return for the rights to put their name on the engine. The Ilmor Formula One engine is a 3.5-liter V-10, which was made obsolete by a rule change a few years ago that limited Formula One engine displacement to 3.0 liters. Nonetheless, that engine and the smaller version in use today share much the same basic design and engineering features.

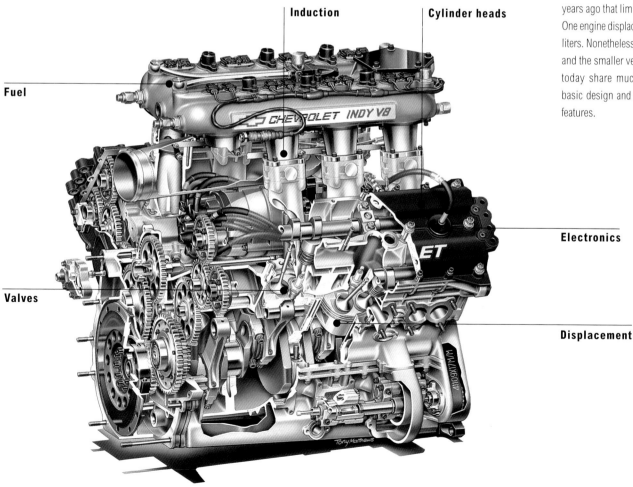

Induction

Cylinder heads

Fuel

Electronics

Valves

Displacement

Valves

Both engines use exotic, lightweight materials for the intake and exhaust valves, there being two of each for each cylinder. Titanium is most often mentioned, although the exact composition is not revealed. The big difference between the engines is the way in which the valves are opened and closed. The Indycar engine uses overhead camshafts that open the valves with the aid of rockers and springs. The Formula One engine employs much more exotic technology, the valves being operated pneumatically. Engine builders went to this technology because the stress placed on valve springs at engine speeds above 10,000 rpm was such that they often failed in race conditions. The pneumatic springs eliminate that problem, but they are very complex and difficult to build.

Cylinder heads

This is one of the most closely-guarded areas of design. The shape of the combustion chamber, whether it's on the Indy engine or the V-12, is one of the major keys to producing power. Perfect burning of all fuel and air, in the right mixture, is the goal, with fuel mileage also in mind. The casting of the heads and machining process are critical, and many designs will be tried over the course of an engine's development.

Induction

The V-10 Formula One engine is known as a naturally-aspirated engine. Its cylinders receive the fuel/air mixture through an airbox on top of the engine that sucks in air without any mechanical aids. The Indy V-8 is allowed to use a turbocharger, which is a pump powered by exhaust gases. This draws in air, puts it under pressure, and rams it into the cylinders with the fuel. One of the basics of engine tuning is that the more fuel/air mixture an engine receives, the more horsepower it can make.

Fuel

The only thing these engines have in common regarding fuel is that they use a lot of it. The Indy engine runs on methanol, which is an alcohol-based fuel, while the Formula One engine uses gasoline, although it is a very high octane blend that is far more powerful than the best street pump fuel.

Electronics

Both engines are equipped with computer-controlled fuel injection, as well as computer controls for spark timing and advance. There is also an array of sensors that monitor combustion chamber temperatures, airflow, and exhaust.

Displacement

The Indy V-8 is limited by the rules to 2.65 liters, which means that the pistons have very short strokes to allow maximum bore. The larger the bore, the more air and fuel you can cram into the combustion chamber, creating more horsepower. Much the same design criterion applies to the 3.5-liter (and the 3.0-liter) Formula One engine. But here, because of the rules, teams are allowed to use as many cylinders as they like to achieve that displacement. The advantage of more cylinders is that it increases the total piston area because the stroke gets smaller. A bigger piston area allows teams to use larger valves, which let in more fuel and air. It's estimated that a V-10 has 7.7 percent more piston area than a V-8, while a V-12 is worth 14.4 percent more. The drawbacks of an engine with more cylinders are that it has many more moving parts — which can create more friction — and it weighs more.

Cylinder heads   **Induction**

Fuel

Valves

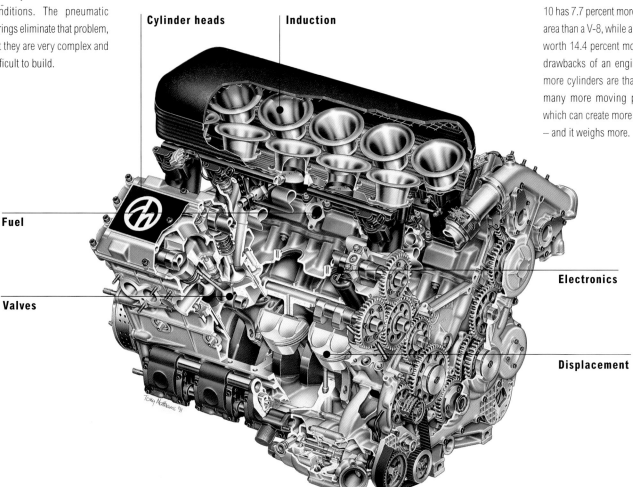

Electronics

Displacement

Ford-Cosworth

The engineering team of Mike Costin and Keith Duckworth came together in 1958 and formed Cosworth Engineering, based in England. Since 1967, when their Ford DFV engine made its debut, the Cosworth name has been a contender in both Formula One and Indycar. At times dominant in each series, Cosworths are on the cutting edge of race car development.

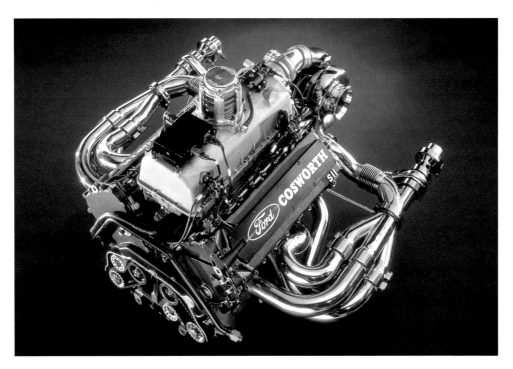

Cosworth XD

Ford-Cosworth is one of the best-known names in racing, both in Formula One and Indycar. This Cosworth XD is the latest design in the Indycar lineage, which can be traced back more than three decades. It is turbocharged, displaces 2.65 liters, and is estimated to produce between 700 and 750 horsepower, depending on the turbo boost setting allowed by race organizers.

Zetec R V-10

Cosworth's answer to the 3.0-liter maximum displacement was the Zetec R V-10. For 1996, this engine is being used by the Sauber team. The output is rated at between 650 and 700 horsepower, and it revs to about 14,000 rpm. Although it has two more cylinders, the smaller-capacity V-10 is down about 100 horsepower from the Zetec V-8.

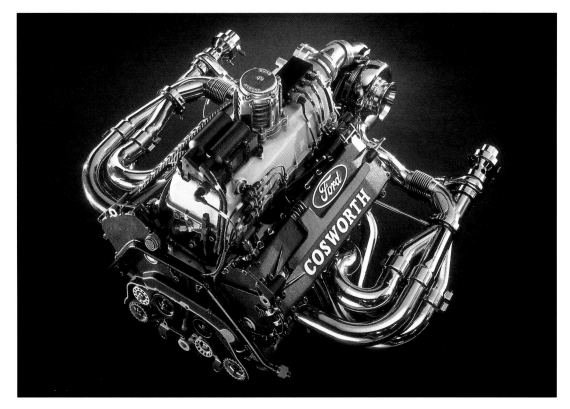

Cosworth XB

This is the Cosworth XB Indycar engine, which was the first Cosworth engine of the 1990s to post a win in the series. It has slightly larger exterior dimensions than the later XD, but displaces the same 2.65 liters. Horsepower was slightly less than the XD, which also benefited from improvements to camshaft profiles and combustion chambers.

Zetec R V-8

The Cosworth Zetec R V-8 was used for several years in Formula One. It powered the Benetton team cars in 1994, and was the last competitive V-8 design in Formula One. Although exact figures were never published by the factory, at its peak it is estimated that the Zetec R V-8 produced as much as 800 horsepower at about 13,500 rpm. When the rules were changed in 1995 to the 3.0-liter displacement limit, the competitiveness of the V-8 design came into question.

Honda

After a brief stab at being a Formula One constructor in the 1960s, and winning only one race, Honda returned to Formula One in the 1980s as an engine supplier to set the winning standard for McLaren. Honda-powered McLarens won successive championships from 1988 to 1991. Honda withdrew from Formula One in 1992, concentrating their efforts on Indycar racing. Although they struggled at the beginning, they posted their first victory in 1995, and in 1996 looked to be one of the dominant engine suppliers.

RA168E Turbo
This is one of Honda's early turbocharged engines that helped set the stage for its long string of victories.

RA100E V-10
This was the first normally-aspirated Honda engine that appeared in 1989 after the Formula One rules banned turbocharged engines in favor of 3.5-liter, non-turbo engines. Honda didn't miss a beat: McLaren Honda won in 1988 with a turbo-powered car, then came back in 1989 to win again under the new rules.

RA121E V-12

The first of the Honda V-12s, this engine appeared in 1991. It was a 60-degree design, and it kept McLaren at the front of the pack.

RA122E V-12

The last of the Honda Grand Prix engines, this 75-degree design was the pinnacle of Honda engineering. It revved to 14,400 rpm, and was conservatively estimated to produce 764 horsepower.

Indy V-8

This is the latest generation of the 2.65-liter Indycar V-8 developed by Honda. More compact in design and lighter than many of its competitors, the Indy V-8 brought Honda its first series win in 1995.

Ilmor Engineering

Like Cosworth, Ilmor Engineering is another British-based company that builds engines for both Formula One and Indycar. The first Ilmor engines to win success in Indycar carried the Chevrolet label, and they were dominant for more than three years, during which time they enjoyed multiple wins at the Indianapolis 500. On the Formula One circuit, Ilmor provide engines for McLaren.

Mercedes-Benz Indy V-8

This engine powers the Penske team and a half-dozen others in the series. It displaces 2.65 liters and is turbocharged, with maximum boost of 45 in. Horsepower is estimated at more than 650.

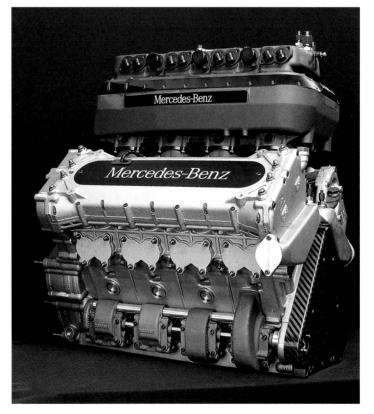

Mercedes-Benz F0110 V-10

McLaren Formula One cars are powered by the Mercedes-Benz F0110 V-10, which is based on a 75-degree cylinder bank design. The 3.0-liter engine is all aluminum with wet cylinder liners.

High-revving

The Mercedes-Benz F0110 V-10 is equipped with pneumatic valve springs and a TAG electronic system that allow it to rev to 16,000 rpm. Horsepower is estimated at above 700.

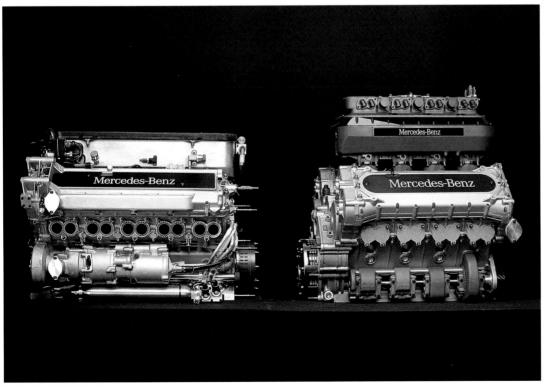

Mercedes-Benz Indy 500 V-8

The taller of these two engines, the Indy 500 V-8, was built especially for the 500-mile classic and took advantage of some special rules for pushrod engines, which are allowed 3.43 liters of displacement and a higher turbo boost level. The result was that Penske's racers were substantially faster than any other cars at the 1994 race, giving a victory to Al Unser Jr. After that race, the engine was retired, and the race organizers changed the rules!

Other makes

Ferrari remains the one team that builds both their engine and chassis, continuing a 40-year tradition. Yamaha, Peugeot, and Renault supply engines to leading Formula One teams such as Williams, Benetton, and Tyrrell.

Peugeot A10 V-10
The Jordan team used Peugeot power exclusively in 1995. The engine was the A10 V-10, which was developed near Paris by Peugeot Sport Engineering.

Renault RS7 V-10
Renault was the engine of choice for the top two teams in 1995 – Benetton and Williams. The Renault RS7 V-10 was a 67-degree design that was capable of producing power up to more than 15,000 rpm. The design was especially light, weighing in at about 290 pounds dry.

Yamaha OX11A V-10

Tyrrell cars are powered by the Yamaha OX11A V-10. This engine represents the work of more than seven years in Formula One competition. It displaces 3.0 liters and employs a 72-degree cylinder block design. Yamaha says it is capable of turning more than 16,000 rpm, and is conservatively rated at more than 650 horsepower.

Ferrari V-12

In the classic Ferrari tradition, a V-12 powered the red Italian machines in 1995. After years of struggling, Ferrari's engine program appeared back on track. The 75-degree design employed 48 valves and was significantly lighter than previous V-12s from Maranello.

Horsepower

There are a great many ways to produce horsepower, as a look at the different engines used in Formula One, Indycar, and NASCAR shows. Although radically different in design, all three types of engine are capable of producing more than 650 horsepower.

Perfect combustion
It would be easy to say that a NASCAR V-8 makes its 650-plus horsepower the old-fashioned way: through cubic inches. However, although the 5.8-liter pushrod engines must make do with cast-iron blocks and carburetors, a lot of science goes into the cylinder heads to produce perfect combustion.

High rpm
This Zetec Formula One engine employs a variety of technologies in its valve train, as well as lightweight material and friction-reducing coatings, to allow it to rev beyond 14,000 rpm. This is the key to a Formula One engine's ability to create horsepower.

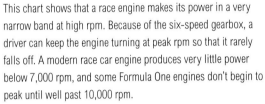

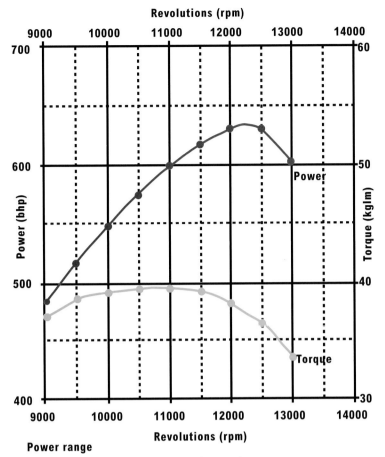

Power range

This chart shows that a race engine makes its power in a very narrow band at high rpm. Because of the six-speed gearbox, a driver can keep the engine turning at peak rpm so that it rarely falls off. A modern race car engine produces very little power below 7,000 rpm, and some Formula One engines don't begin to peak until well past 10,000 rpm.

Turbo boost

With its turbocharger substantially increasing the amount of fuel and air being fed to the cylinders, an Indycar engine can generate tremendous amounts of horsepower from a relatively small-displacement package of just 2.65 liters.

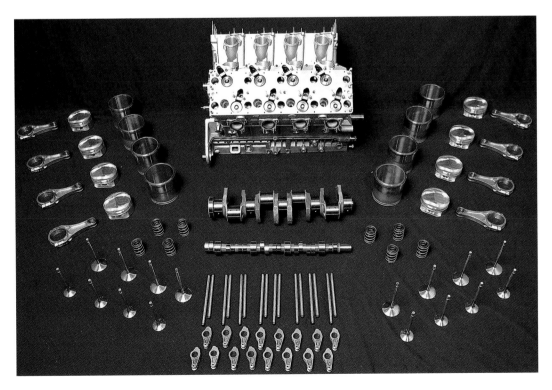

Engineering advances

With many of its pieces laid out, the Mercedes-Benz pushrod V-8 that won the Indianapolis 500 in 1994 looks deceptively simple. It isn't. The engine used a variety of engineering advances to produce more than 750 horsepower at the Brickyard.

Rules and regulations

The sanctioning bodies of the three largest race series – Formula One, Indycar, and NASCAR set very strict guidelines on the specifications for the engines. Some of the rules are intended to help keep costs down and competition close – as in NASCAR – while in Formula One the engine rules are simply general limits under which any new technology can be developed.

Meeting the regulations
Yamaha chose a V-10 configuration to meet the Formula One regulations of no more than 3.0 liters displacement.

Eight cylinders
For many years, the Ford-Cosworth Zetec engines used in Formula One had just eight cylinders to keep the engine's weight, packaging, and reciprocating mass to a minimum.

Indy engine
An Ilmor-Mercedes-Benz Indycar engine, which is turbocharged and displaces 2.65 liters.

Ancient look

A NASCAR engine looks positively prehistoric, not only when compared to engines in other race series, but also to the engines found in modern passenger cars.

Potent engine

This McLaren-Honda V-12, as it raced at Monaco, was one of the most potent engines of its day.

Formula One

All engines must be no more than 3.0 liters in overall displacement and must receive their fuel/air mixture without any external boost. The rules specifically limit the design and opening of the air intake duct so that there can be no internal plumbing to speed up the air, or trap it to build up greater than normal pressure. Teams can have engines with eight, 10, or 12 cylinders configured in any fashion. No other major restrictions exist on engine design, other than a requirement that the engines run on "street pump gasoline."

Indycar

There are three types of engine allowed under the rules, although only two types are currently raced.

The rules allow a turbocharged pushrod engine of no more than 3.43 liters, with a maximum of eight cylinders and two valves per cylinder. The engine is allowed 55 inches of turbo boost pressure. This is called a stock-block arrangement, and is intended to encourage teams to develop engines based on production passenger car engines. Only a Buick-based V-6 has been raced regularly in this configuration. The Mercedes engine, which was raced and was dominant in this configuration at the 1994 Indianapolis 500, was specially built to conform to certain expanded regulations that have since been changed.

The most common engine in Indycar competition is a 2.65-liter, four-valves-per-cylinder, overhead-camshaft design. The maximum number of cylinders is eight, which is what all teams choosing this configuration use. The maximum boost pressure is 45 inches, and there are restrictions on the materials that can be used in the construction of the block, basically limiting teams to aluminum alloys.

A third engine configuration is possible, but at present no teams use this option. It allows a non-turbo, pushrod engine of 5.9 liters, and no more than eight cylinders and two valves per cylinder. The overall size and weight of such an engine would make it uncompetitive in the current chassis configuration.

NASCAR

The only engine available for NASCAR Winston Cup competition is defined as a pushrod V-8 of no more than 5.8 liters that is fed fuel through a carburetor of a specific size and butterfly opening. No electronic injection or other significant electronic control of the engine is allowed. At high-speed tracks, NASCAR installs devices called restrictor plates, which further reduce the amount of fuel that the carburetor can dump into the cylinders, as a way of limiting top speed. Compression ratios are left to the team's

Engine costs

Despite all the attention to chassis development and setup, the single most expensive part of a race car is the engine, especially when on-going development costs are factored in.

In Formula One, the rules are structured so that each team is free to come up with just about any technological advantage that will wring maximum horsepower from the engine. The ultra-competitive nature of the series means that the top teams, which have the sponsors with the deepest pockets, are free to spend enormous amounts of money. At its peak, Honda was rumored to be spending $100 million a year on its Formula One effort, and it's not too far-fetched to say that $50 million a year is a common price paid by other top teams for engine development.

Fourth generation
The Ford-Cosworth XD is the fourth-generation of this design. Although tweaks are made to the Indycar engines throughout the season, it's rare for an all-new engine to appear mid-season.

Exclusive rights
Unlike Indycar, several engine builders supply the teams in Formula One, and many teams have exclusive rights. In this traffic jam at Monaco, engines built by Peugeot, Yamaha, Ford, Renault, Ferrari, and Mercedes-Benz are idle.

In Indycar, the costs are kept considerably below that because the engine formula has been unchanged for many years, meaning that engine builders have not had to use a clean sheet of paper. Also, Indycar engines are restricted in the use of exotic internal materials, as well as such technologies as pneumatic valve openers. In addition, the engine builders not only have a major sponsor (such as Mercedes-Benz or Ford) to underwrite costs in exchange for promotional rights, but they also lease the engines to a number of teams, spreading the costs. An engine lease program can run to about $2.2 million a year per car. At one time, the Ilmor-Chevrolet engine was being used by as many as 20 cars. Figured that way, the engine costs in Indycar are about $50 million, not unlike the cost in Formula One.

The bargain-basement of racing, when it comes to engine costs, is NASCAR. Here, a competitive engine can run as little as $40,000. Over a season, engine costs run to about $200,000, a figure that is kept low because no exotic development work is allowed by the rules.

Engine work
The pit crew works on a Williams car, going over the chassis. The race teams themselves have very little to do with the engine, other than installing it. All engine work is carried out by the engine supplier's own technicians.

The cost
The Renault-powered Williams is one of the fastest cars in Formula One. Its 3.0-liter V-10 engine costs the team as much as $50 million over a single season.

Team of engineers
Damon Hill discusses his car with an engineer. Renault supplies a team of engineers who work with the Williams drivers on the performance of the car's engine.

Fuels

Fuel mileage
The move toward mandatory pit stops in Formula One forced teams to look at fuel in terms of the mileage their cars could achieve in race conditions.

At one time, Formula One was famous for the exotic fuels used by the teams. Many had exclusive arrangements with gasoline suppliers, such as Elf, Shell, Mobil, and Agip, to blend very potent gasolines. The rules stipulated that the octane rating could be no more than 102 RON, and that fuel could contain no more than 1 percent nitrogen and 2 percent oxygen, but made little mention of what else could be included. The chemists at the fuel companies began to develop complex fuels that optimized combustion. It reached the point where specific fuels were developed for qualifying (where higher combustion chamber temperatures and lower fuel mileage could be sustained for short periods) and race conditions. The cost was outrageous, running to more than $400 a gallon by some estimates. Starting in 1992, Formula One teams were ordered to conform to more specific rules that brought racing fuel closer to 102-octane, unleaded pump fuel. It has been reported that the change in fuels initially cost some teams more than 75 horsepower, although since 1992 they have found ways to recoup much of that loss through engine changes.

Methanol
The fuel used in Indycars is not fossil-based like gasoline. It is called methanol and is manufactured for all the teams by Valvoline.

In Indycars, the fuel is not based on gasoline. It is methanol, which is often called wood alcohol and is produced by mixing hydrogen with carbon monoxide under pressure. It has a high energy content, but in the event of fire can be easily extinguished with water. The only safety drawback is that a methanol flame burns clear, so sometimes it may not be apparent that a fire has begun.

NASCAR engines use 110-octane, leaded racing gasoline, which is similar to blends that were available in the 1970s before leaded pump gasoline began to be phased out.

Complex blend
Ayrton Senna sits in the pits in his McLaren. The fuel in his car was supplied by Shell and was a complex blend of agents, but new rules eventually ensured that the fuel was closer to high-octane pump gasoline in make-up.

Special gasoline
McLaren mechanics work on the car prior to qualifying. One of the major advantages the top teams used to have was being able to order special qualifying gasoline that would provide big horsepower boosts for short periods.

Brakes

One of the great failings of race cars was their brakes. After many laps, they would overheat, the brake fluid would absorb moisture and start to boil, and the brake pedal could be floored with no discernible slowing of the car. That still happens occasionally, but the brakes on a modern race car are much more effective. The biggest breakthrough in brakes came during the late 1940s and 1950s with the advent of disc brakes. A disc brake consists of three parts: the rotor, which is a disc that rotates with the wheel; the caliper, which is mounted independently of the rotor and grips it when the brakes are applied; and the pads, which actually come into contact with the rotor when the brakes are applied. In essence, that technology hasn't changed, although improvements have been made to the way in which it is applied and to the materials used. The use of carbon metallic alloys have greatly increased brake effectiveness in high-temperature use such as racing, allowing heat to dissipate quickly when the driver lets off the brakes. This prevents the hydraulic fluid from boiling and rendering the system useless.

Increased cooling

There may be as many as six pistons inside the brake caliper of a Formula One car, and some teams use two calipers to grip the rotor. Also, as a way of increasing cooling of the rotor, it is often drilled with holes that allow air to sweep away heat. Grooves may be cut in some rotors to accomplish much the same thing, and to sweep away any buildup of carbon dust from the pads, which could limit braking efficiency. Both methods also help lighten the brakes.

Exotic materials

A Formula One car's brakes are similar in design to those of an Indycar, but the materials are more exotic and expensive. The rotors are made of carbon-metallic materials, as are the brake pads themselves.

Cast-iron rotors

The rotors on an Indycar are made of cast iron, as defined by the rules. They heat up and cool down very quickly, often reaching more than 1,200°F under hard braking and glowing red hot. After a single race, the rotors will often be discarded because of metal fatigue.

Typical setup

Here is a typical Indycar brake setup. The caliper is either made of cast alloy or machined from a solid billet of metal. Inside the caliper housing are four pistons that are activated hydraulically to press the carbon-metallic brake pads against the rotors. The pistons are drilled with cooling outlets to help dissipate heat. If a caliper reaches above 450°F, the brake fluid will boil.

Gearboxes

As the engine in a Formula One car has evolved into a complex component managed by electronics and computers, so too has the transmission. Since the late 1980s, development work has concentrated on what are called semi-automatic transmissions. These gearboxes use computers and sensors to make sure that the right gear is selected, and that the transmission and engine are running at the correct speed for a smooth shift. Six-speed gearboxes are the norm, but seven-speed gearboxes are coming into use on some circuits. In Indycars, the gearboxes don't have computerized shift aids. They are controlled in a similar manner to a motorcycle gearbox, in which shifts up or down are accomplished by moving the cockpit lever forward or backward, rather than in a traditional H-pattern. A skilled driver can shift gears without using the clutch, thanks to the design of the gearsets in the transmission; all that is needed is a judicious blip of the throttle to equalize engine and gearbox speeds. In addition to providing a range of gears, the transmission serves as a critical chassis member because of the race car's monocoque construction. Rear suspension components and wings are often mounted on the transmission casing. As a result, the gearbox takes a tremendous pounding during a race and, on rough circuits, gearbox failure is not uncommon.

Sturdy, but light
This is the transmission assembly of a Benetton. The springs and dampers for the rear suspension are mounted on top of the gearbox, as is the rear wing. The transmission housing must be stiff enough to withstand the stresses put on it by the wings and suspension, yet be light and compact.

Part of the chassis

The transmission is the rearmost part of the car and is an integral part of the chassis. Most gearboxes are mounted transversely — meaning across the car, rather than along its axis — to decrease the overall length of the racer. This is quite critical with V-10 and V-12 engines, which are longer to accommodate more cylinders than a V-8.

Compact unit

A Formula One transmission is a compact unit, its overall length being dictated by the chassis design. The clutch is a dual-plate, carbon metallic design that is only actuated by the driver on moving away from a standing start.

Cockpit ergonomics

Shifting gears in a race car used to be an art form. It was the matching of engine speed with the speed of the rear wheels, and when done properly in a turn, it was a great feat. The old technique was called "heel-and-toe," in which the driver blipped the throttle with one part of his right foot to maintain peak revs, while applying the brake with another part of his foot. The shift lever travelled in an H pattern, and was moved up, back, and across to row through the gears. In today's Formula One machines, the traditional gear lever has been replaced by paddles on the steering wheel that tell the semi-automatic gearbox when to shift. A more traditional shift lever can be found in Indycars, mounted to the side of the driver's seat. But it's a sequential shifter, much like that used on most motorcycles, rather than having a traditional H-pattern. The only place you'll find a traditional four-speed, H-pattern gearbox is in NASCAR, but on most of their tracks the cars remain in top gear for all but the pit stops. However, despite all the high-tech wonders of the modern race car, two things are still left up to the driver: the shapes of the seat and the steering wheel.

No more missed shifts

With his hands free from having to work an H-pattern shifter to select the proper gear, Damon Hill can concentrate on working the best line through a turn in his Williams. The semi-automatic gearbox has made missed shifts a thing of the past.

Side-mounted

The gear shift lever on this Honda-powered Indycar is mounted at the side of the cockpit, next to the seat. It is a simple forward-backward lever. If a driver is in fifth gear and wants third, he just pulls back twice on the lever.

Molded seat

In this 1996 Reynard, the seat is molded specifically to fit the body profile of the driver, in this case Raul Boesel. This ensures that the shift lever, and gas, brake, and clutch pedals are all within easy reach at race speeds.

Changing style
The shift paddles are mounted behind the steering wheel in this Formula One cockpit. Note the style of the steering wheel, which can vary from an airplane-like half-wheel to a rectangular full wheel.

Facts and Figures

FIA FORMULA 1 WORLD DRIVING CHAMPIONSHIP

YEAR	DRIVER	COUNTRY	CAR-ENGINE
1950	Giuseppe Farina	Italy	Alfa-Romeo 158/159 sc
1951	Juan Manuel Fangio	Argentina	Alfa-Romeo 159 sc
1952	Alberto Ascari	Italy	Ferrari 500
1953	Alberto Ascari	Italy	Ferrari 500
1954	Juan Manuel Fangio	Argentina	Mercedes-Benz W196/ Maserati 250F
1955	Juan Manuel Fangio	Argentina	Mercedes-Benz W196
1956	Juan Manuel Fangio	Argentina	Lancia-Ferrari D50
1957	Juan Manuel Fangio	Argentina	Maserati 250F
1958	Mike Hawthorn	Great Britain	Ferrari Dino 246
1959	Jack Brabham	Australia	Cooper-Climax T51
1960	Jack Brabham	Australia	Cooper-Climax T53
1961	Phil Hill	United States	Ferrari Dino 156
1962	Graham Hill	Great Britain	BRM P57
1963	Jim Clark	Great Britain	Lotus-Climax 25
1964	John Surtees	Great Britain	Ferrari 158
1965	Jim Clark	Great Britain	Lotus-Climax 33
1966	Jack Brabham	Australia	Brabham-Repco BT19/BT20
1967	Denny Hulme	New Zealand	Brabham-Repco BT20/BT24
1968	Graham Hill	Great Britain	Lotus-Ford 49/49B
1969	Jackie Stewart	Great Britain	Matra-Ford MS10/MS80
1970	Jochen Rindt	Austria	Lotus-Ford 49C/72
1971	Jackie Stewart	Great Britain	Tyrrell-Ford 001/003
1972	Emerson Fittipaldi	Brazil	Lotus-Ford 72
1973	Jackie Stewart	Great Britain	Tyrrell-Ford 005/006
1974	Emerson Fittipaldi	Brazil	McLaren-Ford M23
1975	Niki Lauda	Austria	Ferrari 312T
1976	James Hunt	Great Britain	McLaren-Ford M23
1977	Niki Lauda	Austria	Ferrari 312T2
1978	Mario Andretti	United States	Lotus-Ford 78/79
1979	Jody Scheckter	South Africa	Ferrari 312T3/312T4
1980	Alan Jones	Australia	Williams-Ford FW07B
1981	Nelson Piquet	Brazil	Brabham-Ford BT49C
1982	Keke Rosberg	Finland	Williams-Ford FW07C/FW08
1983	Nelson Piquet	Brazil	Brabham-BMW BT52/BT52B tc
1984	Niki Lauda	Austria	McLaren-TAG Porsche MP4/2 tc
1985	Alain Prost	France	McLaren-TAG Porsche MP4/2B tc
1986	Alain Prost	France	McLaren-TAG Porsche MP4/2C tc
1987	Nelson Piquet	Brazil	Williams-Honda FW11B tc
1988	Ayrton Senna	Brazil	McLaren-Honda MP4/4 tc
1989	Alain Prost	France	McLaren-Honda MP4/5
1990	Ayrton Senna	Brazil	McLaren-Honda MP4/5B
1991	Ayrton Senna	Brazil	McLaren-Honda MP4/6
1992	Nigel Mansell	Great Britain	Williams-Renault FW14
1993	Alain Prost	France	Williams-Renault FW15
1994	Michael Schumacher	Germany	Benetton-Ford B194
1995	Michael Schumacher	Germany	Benetton-Renault B195

FIA FORMULA 1 CONSTRUCTOR'S WORLD CHAMPIONSHIP

YEAR	CONSTRUCTOR
1958	Vanwall
1959	Cooper-Climax
1960	Cooper-Climax
1961	Ferrari
1962	BRM
1963	Lotus-Climax
1964	Ferrari
1965	Lotus-Climax
1966	Brabham-Repco
1967	Brabham-Repco
1968	Lotus-Ford
1969	Matra-Ford
1970	Lotus-Ford
1971	Tyrrell-Ford
1972	Lotus-Ford
1973	Lotus-Ford
1974	McLaren-Ford
1975	Ferrari
1976	Ferrari
1977	Ferrari
1978	Lotus-Ford
1979	Ferrari
1980	Williams-Ford
1981	Williams-Ford
1982	Ferrari
1983	Ferrari
1984	McLaren-TAG Porsche
1985	McLaren-TAG Porsche
1986	Williams-Honda
1987	Williams-Honda
1988	McLaren-Honda
1989	McLaren-Honda
1990	McLaren-Honda
1991	McLaren-Honda
1992	Williams-Renault
1993	Williams-Renault
1994	Williams-Renault
1995	Benetton-Renault

FORMULA 1 GRAND PRIX WINNERS

POS.	DRIVER	COUNTRY	WINS
1	Alain Prost	France	51
2	Ayrton Senna	Brazil	41
3	Nigel Mansell	Great Britain	31
4	Jackie Stewart	Great Britain	27
5	Jim Clark	Great Britain	25
	Niki Lauda	Austria	25
7	Juan Manuel Fangio	Argentina	24
8	Nelson Piquet	Brazil	23
9	Michael Schumacher	Germany	17*
10	Stirling Moss	Great Britain	16
11	Jack Brabham	Australia	14
	Emerson Fittipaldi	Brazil	14
	Graham Hill	Great Britain	14
14	Alberto Ascari	Italy	13
15	Mario Andretti	United States	12
	Damon Hill	Great Britain	12*
	Alan Jones	Australia	12
	Carlos Reutemann	Argentina	12
19	James Hunt	Great Britain	10
	Ronnie Peterson	Sweden	10
	Jody Scheckter	South Africa	10
22	Gerhard Berger	Austria	8*
	Denny Hulme	New Zealand	8
	Jacky Ickx	Belgium	8
25	Rene Arnoux	France	7
26	Tony Brooks	Great Britain	6
	Jacques Laffite	France	6
	Riccardo Patrese	Italy	6
	Jochen Rindt	Austria	6
	John Surtees	Great Britain	6
	Gilles Villeneuve	Canada	6
32	Michele Alboreto	Italy	5
	Giuseppe Farina	Italy	5
	Clay Regazzoni	Switzerland	5
	Keke Rosberg	Finland	5
	John Watson	Great Britain	5
37	Dan Gurney	United States	4
	Bruce McLaren	New Zealand	4
39	Thierry Boutsen	Belgium	3
	Peter Collins	Great Britain	3
	Mike Hawthorn	Great Britain	3
	Phil Hill	United States	3
	Didier Pironi	France	3
44	Elio de Angelis	Italy	2
45	Johnny Herbert	Great Britain	2*
46	Jean Alesi	France	1*
	David Coulthard	Great Britain	1*

*Active driver

Wins through the 1995 season.

CURRENT DRIVER	TEAM
Damon Hill	Williams-Renault
Michael Schumacher	Ferrari
Jean Alesi	Benetton-Renault
Jacques Villeneuve	Williams-Renault
Gerhard Berger	Benetton-Renault
Heinz-Harald Frentzen	McLaren-Mercedes
Eddie Irvine	Ferrari
Mika Hakkinen	McLaren-Mercedes
David Coulthard	McLaren-Mercedes
Johnny Herbert	Sauber-Ford
Rubens Barrichello	Jordan-Peugeot
Jos Verstappen	Footwork-Hart
Gianni Morbidelli	Footwork-Hart
Mika Salo	Tyrrell-Yamaha
Olivier Panis	Ligier-Mugen
Ukyo Katayama	Tyrrell-Yamaha
Luca Badoer	Minardi-Ford
Pedro Lamy	Minardi-Ford
Pedro Diniz	Ligier-Mugen
Taki Inoue	Forti-Ford

INDY 500 CHAMPIONS

Note: 1917–18 No races, World War I
    1942–45 No races, World War II

YEAR	DRIVER	COUNTRY	(MPH)	(KPH)
1911	Ray Harroun	United States	74.59	120.04
1912	Joe Dawson	United States	78.72	126.60
1913	Jules Goux	France	75.93	122.20
1914	Rene Thomas	France	82.47	132.72
1915	Ralph DePalma	Italy	89.84	144.58
1916	Dario Resta	Italy	84.00	135.18
1919	Howard Wilcox	United States	88.05	141.70
1920	Gaston Chevrolet	France	88.62	142.62
1921	Tommy Milton	United States	89.62	144.23
1922	Jimmy Murphy	United States	94.48	152.05
1923	Tommy Milton	United States	90.95	146.37
1924	L. L. Corum and Joe Boyer	United States	98.23	158.09
1925	Pete DePaolo	United States	98.23	158.09
1926	Frank Lochart	United States	95.90	154.34
1927	George Souders	United States	97.55	156.99
1928	Louis Meyer	United States	99.48	160.10
1929	Ray Keech	United States	97.59	157.06
1930	Billy Arnold	United States	100.45	161.66
1931	Louis Schneider	United States	96.63	155.51
1932	Fred Frame	United States	104.14	167.60
1933	Louis Meyer	United States	104.16	167.63
1934	Bill Cummings	United States	104.86	168.76
1935	Kelly Petillo	United States	106.24	170.98
1936	Louis Meyer	United States	109.07	175.53
1937	Wilbur Shaw	United States	113.58	182.79
1938	Floyd Roberts	United States	117.20	188.62
1939	Wilbur Shaw	United States	115.04	185.14
1940	Wilbur Shaw	United States	114.28	183.92
1941	Floyd Davis and Mauri Rose	United States	115.12	185.27
1946	George Robson	Great Britain	114.82	184.78
1947	Mauri Rose	United States	116.34	187.23
1948	Mauri Rose	United States	119.81	192.82
1949	Bill Holland	United States	121.33	195.26
1950	Johnnie Parsons	United States	124.00	199.56
1951	Lee Wallard	United States	126.24	203.16
1952	Troy Ruttman	United States	128.92	207.48
1953	Bill Vukovich, Sr.	United States	128.74	207.19
1954	Bill Vukovich, Sr.	United States	130.84	210.57
1955	Bob Sweikert	United States	128.21	206.33
1956	Pat Flaherty	United States	128.49	206.78
1957	Sam Hanks	United States	135.60	218.23
1958	Jimmy Bryan	United States	133.79	215.31
1959	Rodger Ward	United States	135.86	218.65
1960	Jim Rathmann	United States	138.77	223.33
1961	A. J. Foyt, Jr.	United States	139.13	223.91
1962	Rodger Ward	United States	140.29	225.77
1963	Parnelli Jones	United States	143.14	230.36
1964	A. J. Foyt, Jr.	United States	147.35	237.14
1965	Jimmy Clark	Great Britain	150.69	242.51
1966	Graham Hill	Great Britain	144.32	232.26
1967	A. J. Foyt, Jr.	United States	151.21	243.35
1968	Bobby Unser	United States	152.88	246.04
1969	Mario Andretti	United States	156.87	252.46
1970	Al Unser, Sr.	United States	155.75	250.66
1971	Al Unser, Sr.	United States	157.74	253.86
1972	Mark Donohue	United States	162.96	262.26
1973	Gordon Johncock	United States	159.04	255.95
1974	Johnny Rutherford	United States	158.59	255.22
1975	Bobby Unser	United States	149.21	240.13
1976	Johnny Rutherford	United States	158.59	255.22
1977	A. J. Foyt, Jr.	United States	149.21	240.13
1978	Al Unser, Sr.	United States	161.36	259.64
1979	Rick Mears	United States	158.90	255.72
1980	Johnny Rutherford	United States	142.86	229.87
1981	Bobby Unser	United States	139.08	223.83
1982	Gordon Johncock	United States	162.03	260.76
1983	Tom Sneva	United States	162.12	260.90
1984	Rick Mears	United States	163.61	263.30
1985	Danny Sullivan	United States	152.98	246.20
1986	Bobby Rahal	United States	170.72	274.75
1987	Al Unser, Sr.	United States	162.18	261.00
1988	Rick Mears	United States	144.81	233.05
1989	Emerson Fittipaldi	Brazil	167.58	269.69
1990	Arie Luyendyk	Netherlands	185.98	299.31
1991	Rick Mears	United States	176.46	283.98
1992	Al Unser, Jr.	United States	134.48	216.42
1993	Emerson Fittipaldi	Brazil	148.65	239.55
1994	Al Unser, Jr.	United States	160.87	259.05
1995	Jacques Villeneuve	Canada	153.62	247.37

ACTIVE INDYCAR RACING TEAMS

All-American Racers
Team owner: Dan Gurney
Drivers: Juan Manuel Fangio II, P. J. Jones
Car/engine/tires: 1996 Eagle/Toyota/Goodyear

Areiero Wells Racing
Team owners: Frank Areiero, Cal Wells III
Driver: Jeff Krosnoff
Car/engine/tires: 1996 Reynard/Toyota/Firestone

Bettenhausen Motorsports/Team Alumax
Team owner: Tony Bettenhausen
Driver: Stefan Johansson
Car/engine/tires: 1996 Reynard/Mercedes-Benz/Goodyear

Brahma Sports Team
Team owner: Barry Green
Driver: Raul Boesel
Car/engine/tires: 1996 Reynard/Ford-Cosworth/Goodyear

Brix Comptech Racing
Team owners: Harry Brix, Don Erb, Doug Peterson
Driver: Parker Johnstone
Car/engine/tires: 1996 Reynard/Honda/Firestone

Delco Electronics High Tech Team Galles
Team owner: Rick Galles
Driver: Eddie Lawson
Car/engine/tires: 1996 Lola/Mercedes-Benz/Goodyear

Derrick Walker Racing
Team owner: Derrick Walker
Drivers: Robby Gordon, Scott Goodyear
Car/engine/tires: 1996 Reynard/Ford-Cosworth/Goodyear

Hall Racing
Team owner: Jim Hall
Driver: Gil de Ferran
Car/engine/tires: 1996 Reynard/Honda/Goodyear

Hogan Penske Racing
Team owners: Carl Hogan, Roger Penske
Driver: Emerson Fittipaldi
Car/engine/tires: 1996 Penske/Mercedes-Benz/Goodyear

Marlboro Team Penske
Team owner: Roger Penske
Drivers: Al Unser Jr, Paul Tracy
Car/engine/tires: 1996 Penske/Mercedes-Benz/Goodyear

Newman/Haas Racing
Team owners: Paul Newman, Carl Haas
Drivers: Michael Andretti, Christian Fittipaldi
Car/engine/tires: 1996 Lola/Ford-Cosworth/Goodyear

Pac West Racing Group
Team owners: Bruce R. McCaw, Tom Armstrong, Dominic Dobson, Wes Lematta
Drivers: Mauricio Gugelmin, Mark Blundell
Car/engine/tires: 1996 Reynard/Ford-Cosworth/Goodyear

Patrick Racing
Team owner: U. E. "Pat" Patrick

Driver: Scott Pruett
Car/engine/tires: 1996 Lola/Ford-Cosworth/Firestone

Payton Coyne Racing
Team owners: Walter Payton, Dale Coyne
Driver: Hiro Matsushita
Car/engine/tires: 1996 Lola/Ford-Cosworth/Firestone

Player's Ltd/Forsythe Racing
Team owner: Gerald Forsythe
Driver: Greg Moore
Car/engine/tires: 1995 Reynard/Mercedes-Benz/Firestone

Target/Chip Ganassi Racing
Team owner: Chip Ganassi
Drivers: Jimmy Vasser, Alex Zanardi
Car/engine/tires: 1996 Reynard/Honda/Firestone

Tasman Motorsports Group
Team owners: Steve Horne, Jeffrey Eischen, Ben Dillon, Stanley Ross
Drivers: Andre Ribeiro, Adrian Fernandez
Car/engine/tires: 1996 Lola/Honda/Firestone

Team Rahal
Team owners: Bobby Rahal, David Letterman
Drivers: Bobby Rahal, Bryan Herta
Car/engine/tires: 1996 Reynard/Mercedes-Benz/Goodyear

Team Scandia
Team owners: Andy and Ann Evans
Driver: Elisco Salazar
Car/engine/tires: 1996 Lola/Ford-Cosworth/Goodyear

NASCAR CHAMPIONS

YEAR	DRIVER	MAKE
1949	Red Byron	Oldsmobile
1950	Bill Rexford	Oldsmobile
1951	Herb Thomas	Hudson
1952	Tim Flock	Hudson
1953	Herb Thomas	Hudson
1954	Lee Petty	Chrysler
1955	Tim Flock	Chrysler
1956	Buck Baker	Chrysler
1957	Buck Baker	Chevrolet
1958	Lee Petty	Oldsmobile
1959	Lee Petty	Plymouth
1960	Rex White	Chevrolet
1961	Ned Jarrett	Chevrolet
1962	Joe Weatherly	Pontiac
1963	Joe Weatherly	Mercury
1964	Richard Petty	Plymouth
1965	Ned Jarrett	Ford
1966	David Pearson	Dodge
1967	Richard Petty	Plymouth
1968	David Pearson	Ford
1969	David Pearson	Ford
1970	Bobby Isaac	Dodge
1971	Richard Petty	Plymouth
1972	Richard Petty	Plymouth
1973	Benny Parsons	Chevrolet
1974	Richard Petty	Dodge
1975	Richard Petty	Dodge
1976	Cale Yarborough	Chevrolet
1977	Cale Yarborough	Chevrolet
1978	Cale Yarborough	Oldsmobile
1979	Richard Petty	Chevrolet
1980	Dale Earnhardt	Chevrolet
1981	Darrell Waltrip	Buick
1982	Darrell Waltrip	Buick
1983	Bobby Allison	Buick
1984	Terry Labonte	Chevrolet
1985	Darrell Waltrip	Chevrolet
1986	Dale Earnhardt	Chevrolet
1987	Dale Earnhardt	Chevrolet
1988	Bill Elliott	Ford
1989	Rusty Wallace	Pontiac
1990	Dale Earnhardt	Chevrolet
1991	Dale Earnhardt	Chevrolet
1992	Alan Kulwicki	Ford
1993	Dale Earnhardt	Chevrolet
1994	Dale Earnhardt	Chevrolet
1995	Jeff Gordon	Chevrolet

A glossary of racing terms

A-arms These are the suspension components that run from the race car tub or rear transmission housing to the wheels. They are called A-arms because of their design – wide where they attach to the chassis, with a narrow point where they attach to the wheels. The length of the A-arms determines suspension and steering response.

Active suspension A form of Formula One suspension that used electronic sensors and special shock absorbers to change the suspension stiffness to match road surfaces. Very expensive, active suspension made a car much easier to control in corners, especially on a bumpy surface. It was banned because of concerns that only the richest Formula One teams could afford the technology.

Aerodynamics The science of how a body moves through the air. As it applies to race cars, it is the science of using the airflow to enhance cornering and braking capabilities without limiting straight-line speed. *See also* Downforce.

Apex The point in a turn where it is at its greatest angle. On a race track, the apex is the point where the race car should just skim the inner portion of the track while accelerating toward the next straightaway.

Calipers The disc brake housing and pistons that grip the brake rotor. The pistons are pushed against the rotor hydraulically. The calipers are prone to heat buildup during hard racing, which can cause the brake fluid to boil and the brake system to fail.

Carbon fiber A space-age material, made from a carbon composite bonded with a resin, that is lighter than fiberglass or aluminum honeycomb, yet many times stronger. It has the advantage of being suitable for molding into complex shapes, such as body shells or chassis tubs. It also shatters in a severe crash in such a way as to dissipate energy away from the driver, helping lessen injuries and deaths.

Carburetor A mechanical fuel delivery device that has been replaced by computer-controlled fuel injection in all major forms of racing except NASCAR.

Dampers Also called shock absorbers, these liquid- or gas-filled tubes help control the movement of the suspension when the car is riding over uneven surfaces. On a modern race car, the oil for the dampers is usually carried in a separate reservoir, unlike a passenger car damper, which is a self-contained unit.

Downforce The desirable effect when air is directed over a race car in such a way as to increase the force holding it to the track. Downforce is usually created by wings and pods. It is not unusual for a modern race car to develop more than twice its weight in downforce.

Drafting The racing technique of pulling up close to the car in front and taking advantage of the hole it cuts in the air. Since the trailing car doesn't have to work as hard against air resistance, it can often gain enough momentum to pull out and pass the lead car. This technique works best in NASCAR.

Drag coefficient This is the measurement of the amount of wind resistance a car presents due to its shape. An open-wheeled race car has a relatively high drag coefficient when compared to a street car, in large part because of the uncovered wheels and the big wings. Although a race car needs to cut through the air as cleanly as possible, it also strives to grab the air and use it to help increase track grip.

Engine Management System A general term applied to the computers and sensors that control all of the engine functions, such as fuel delivery, airflow, and spark advance. It can also refer to the auxiliary system that downloads data to the pit crew. It is often called "the black box."

Formula One The name applied to the top technological form of racing in the world. Also called Grand Prix cars, Formula One racers are built under a set of guidelines that allow a large degree of experimentation. Such experimentation leads to enormous costs, and Formula One is acknowledged to be the most expensive form of racing.

Ground effects A term that applies to a way of managing airflow so that a vacuum is created underneath a car that sucks it close to the ground. Some Formula One teams went to extremes to create ground effects, even using fans to suck the air from beneath the car. Some passive forms of ground effects are still used today, but the rules are continually being changed to restrict its effectiveness out of concern for safety. When a ground effects car loses its grip on the track, it can become uncontrollable quickly.

Indycar The premier open-wheel racing series in the United States, named for the Indianapolis 500, which is the crown jewel of the series. In 1995, the series was challenged by the Indy Racing League, which was founded by the owner of the Indianapolis Motor Speedway.

Kevlar A light, but strong, composite material that is a form of carbon fiber. It is often used in race car chassis construction.

Lift What happens when air pressure builds up beneath a race car's wings at high speed. It can cause a car to lose traction and spin out, but usually can be cured by an adjustment of the wings.

Loose A term applied to the rear end of a car that slides in a turn. It is used largely by NASCAR drivers. *See also* Oversteer.

Methanol Fuel burned by Indycars. It is a chemical-based fuel that is produced by combining alcohol and carbon monoxide under pressure.

Monocoque A form of chassis construction that is prevalent in Formula One and Indycar. A monocoque chassis uses its major components – cockpit tub, engine, transmission – as the basis of the car, rather than having a separate frame onto which all those components are mounted.

NASCAR The sanctioning body founded by Bill France Sr., who built the Daytona International Speedway. It oversees the Winston Cup series, which is the most popular racing series in the United States.

Naturally aspirated This term refers to the manner in which air reaches the combustion chambers of the engine. A naturally-aspirated engine has no mechanical aids to increase air pressure above the ambient level. *See also* Turbocharging.

Oversteer A handling condition in which the rear end of a car tends to lose traction and spin out. The mirror image of understeer. *See also* Loose.

Pit control The electronic hub of a race team at the track. Computers receive telemetry from the race car and download it to engineers, who can assess a car's performance during a race or practice, then make necessary adjustments.

Pneumatic Valve Springs A high-tech method of opening and closing the valves in a Formula One engine. The complex arrangement was developed because standard valve springs cannot withstand the stresses of operation at engine speeds that can reach 16,000 rpm.

Push A handling condition in which the front wheels lack traction and the car tends to continue in a straight line, even though the wheels are turned. At some point in a race, most race cars exhibit some degree of push. *See also* Understeer.

Pyrometer A heat sensor used to measure the surface temperature at three points across the face of a race tire immediately after leaving the track. These readings can indicate to an engineer the type of chassis adjustments to make.

Radial tires These race tires are constructed so that the tire cords run radially around the casing. This type of construction improves the grip of the tread on the road, while the sidewall absorbs lateral forces under cornering.

Rain tires These are treaded, soft-compound tires for use when the racing surface becomes wet. The tread helps channel water from under the tire, improving traction. When the track is dry, however, the soft compound of these tires – combined with the heat buildup in the tread – makes them

uncompetitive, and teams must switch back to the slick tires, which are superior on dry pavement.

Red line A term that refers to the maximum revolutions at which an engine can be run without risking failure. The red line on many Formula One engines is in excess of 14,000 rpm.

Rotors The solid discs that the brake calipers grab to slow down a car. On Indycars, the rotors are of cast iron, while in Formula One, they are of a carbon composite. The temperature of a brake rotor can easily exceed 1,200°F under hard braking, then drop to 200°F when the brakes are released.

Semi-automatic gearbox A transmission in which electronic controls actually make the shifts, regulating engine speed and clutch operation. This type of gearbox is only allowed in Formula One.

The line Theoretically, the fastest way around a turn. The line can often be seen on a race track as the heavy rubber buildup left by a continual stream of race cars over a narrow stretch of pavement.

Turbocharging A method of increasing the amount and pressure of fuel and air fed to an engine. A turbocharger is a pump that is turned by exhaust gases. The pump sucks in air and forces it into the combustion chambers with the fuel, at a far greater pressure than normal, increasing power.

Understeer A handling term that refers to a car's tendency to continue in a straight line when the wheels are turned. *See also* Push.

V-8, V-10, V-12 The three most popular engine layouts in racing, each having two banks of cylinders arranged in a V-configuration. The cant of the V-angle varies according to the engine builder, but in general the banks of cylinders are set at an angle between 60 and 75 degrees. V-8s are common in Indycars, while V-10s and V-12s are only seen in Formula One cars.

Wickerbill A small, adjustable lip on the trailing edge of a race car wing that directs airflow smoothly off the wing surface, helping to create greater downforce.

Wings Large airfoils at the front and back of an open-wheel race car that generate tremendous amounts of downforce, particularly at high speeds.

Index Italic page numbers refer to picture captions

Picture credits

The author and publishers wish to thank the following for permission to reproduce illustrations.

Jennifer Podis '96
23, 25b, 27, 29t, 35tl,br, 36r, 37b, 39tr, 51br, 57bl, 61, 62, 63, 70, 73t, 78b, 79, 85, 95, 110t, 115, 118br

Sutton Motorsport Images
6r, 41r, 50, 59m, 69t, 74, 77, 81m, 84b, 89br, 90, 92, 105b, 114t, 116, 117b, 123, 86, 87, 92r

Zooom Photographic
13b, 19b, 24, 25tm, 26, 30, 5bl, 36l, 37t, 40, 41, 56, 57br, 58, 63tr, 71b, 73, 75b, 78t, 81b, 102t, 104, 108tl,tr, 112
Darren Heath Zooom Photographic
30, 31, 39br
David Winter Zooom Photographic

Harold Barker
7b
Lotus
7t, 32, 33

ICN Co-ordination
8, 18, 46b, 75t, 82b, 88bl, 118t, 121bl

Dan R. Boyd
12, 13t, 19t, 42, 51

EMPICS Ltd
14, 16t, 59t, 64, 82t, 89bl, 110b, 111

Rothmans
15t, 16b, 20, 22, 35tr, 39tl, 46t, 47, 48b, 49b, 54, 69m, 72, 83

Honda
15b, 17, 34, 49t, 57t, 68, 88t,br, 89t, 100, 101, 109b, 113, 114b, 117t, 118bl,119, 121t

International Speedway Corp. (ISC Photo)
19m, 59b

Marlboro
48t, 69b

Reynard
52

Toyota
53

t=top, b=bottom, m=middle, l=left, r=right

DESIGN BRIEFS

LOLA T93/20
A Fresh Start

■ This is an important year for Indy Lights. After seven rather lean years, it is hoped that a new car from Lola will help bring some depth and vitality to the category. There's also the increasingly desperate economic situation in Europe, with Formula 3000 due to be replaced in 1994 with a restricted, stock-block-type formula roughly similar to Indy Lights. European defectors have bolstered Indy Lights fields since the formula's beginnings in 1986, and that trend is expected to expand this year to include teams as well as drivers.

The original March F3000-based car will be replaced over the next two years by a new Lola F3000-based chassis. The Lola T93/20 Indy Lights is powered by the familiar 425hp, 4.2-liter Buick V6, and is more modern technically and more appealing visually than the aging March chassis that have remained unchanged—save for bodywork revisions—since 1986.

The T93/20 is based on a current F3000 carbon chassis with aluminum bulkheads that has been beefed up to improve crashability on ovals. "We're not concerned about saving weight," commented Indy Lights president Roger Bailey. "We're concerned about safety."

More carbon is built into the front of the chassis in particular, which is taller and wider than its F3000 brethren. Inserts have also been added to raise the height of the cockpit sides to guard against wheel intrusion in high-speed oval accidents. The chassis has been crash-tested at England's Cranfield Institute, where it passed FISA's impact regulations.

Costs have been reduced at the expense of some weight in things like front wings. These carbon pieces have been constructed in wet lay-up rather than

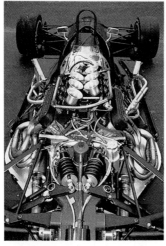

pre-preg, but because the car won't have to meet the 1190lb F3000 weight minimum, there are no weight worries. In fact, the T93/20 is some 130lb heavier than Lola's latest F3000 car.

Compared to the existing March Indy Lights cars, the new car should generate considerably more downforce because the tail wing on the new car reaches both higher and farther back. There's also a lower, sleeker tail to aid airflow to the wing.

The T93/20 should also benefit from new six-pot brakes. These will theoretically make for more even pad wear and better braking. It is also a stouter gearbox than the March. The transmission has

been built around Hewland's TPT internals, as used in many current F1 cars. Though smaller in diameter than DG-type Indy car gears, the TPT gears are larger than the old March/Hewland FGBs.

Lola's 25-man engineering team contributed to the new Indy Lights car, with Eric Broadley's son Andrew leading the project. Andrew has spent the past two racing seasons in the USA, and will oversee pre-season testing of the T93/20. Full customer support will be supplied at the races by a Carl Haas parts truck, while Lola's Michigan-based U.S. liaison, Neil Mickleright, attends all races and will extend his reach to include Indy Lights.

Just before Christmas, Roger Bailey reported that 30 deposits had been received for T93/20s. Twelve cars had been completed by Lola, and were ready for ship-

ping to the USA. Another 10 are planned for construction in February, after the primary batch of new T93/00 Indy cars is built.

"After that, we'll just keep building the cars as necessary," commented Bailey. "My feeling is we'll have 26 to 28 cars out there, including a handful of old cars. To be truthful, if we have 20 cars at every race, we'll be happy."

Sponsorship of the series continues from tire supplier Firestone and engine supplier Buick, as well as PPG. The 12-race Firestone Indy Lights championship runs, as always, in conjunction with IndyCar races. Prize

NEW DEAL
Requisite Indy Lights Buick V6 engine (FAR LEFT) will call a brand-new Lola chassis (TOP) home in '93. Adapted from Lola's F3000 car, with safety and cost-saving modifications, the T93/20 features wishbone-pushrod suspension both front and rear (LEFT).

money continues at $70,000 per race, with $20,000 to win. There's a further $175,000 in year-end awards. Each race is televised on a delayed basis by ESPN, with a half-hour show aired approximately two weeks later.

Among this year's championship favorites is Franck Freon, who has moved from Landford to John Martin's team. Also highly rated is Bryan Herta, who will lead Steve Horne's two-car TMG team. Among the newcomers to the series will be USAC FF2000 champion Greg Moore. —*Gordon Kirby*

SPECIFICATIONS

Front/Rear track	67.22in./62.54in.
Wheelbase	111.0in.
Overall width/length	77.2in./ 179in.
Overall height (from floor)	35.5in.
Front wheels	15in. diam. X 10in. wide
Rear wheels	15in. diam. X 14in. wide
Fuel tank capacity	34 U.S. gal
Weight	1320lb

PHOTOGRAPHY by SUTTON PHOTOGRAPHIC

LEGEND All times listed are for Eastern Time Zone. Times accurate at time of printing, but check your local listings for any changes.

L = Live program   R = Repeat program

ESPN=Entertainment and Sports Programming Network
RDS=Le Reseau Des Sports (Cdn.)   **TBS**=Turner Broadcasting Network
TNN=The Nashville Network   **TSN**=The Sports Network (Cdn.)

JAN. 24–MAR. 6

SUNDAY JANUARY 31

■ TODAY'S EVENTS

IMSA Camel GT Series, Rolex 24 at Daytona, Daytona Beach, Fla.
IMSA Camel Lights, Rolex 24 at Daytona, Daytona Beach, Fla.
IMSA Exxon Supreme Series, Rolex 24 at Daytona, Daytona Beach, Fla.

■ RACING ON TV

8:30am R	Motoring '93	TSN
10:00am	Winners: Willy T. Ribbs	TNN
10:30am	NIIRA Today	TNN
11:00am	Inside Winston Cup Racing	TNN
11:30am L	Raceday	TNN
3:30pm	NHRA Today	TNN
3:30pm R	NHRA Budweiser Top Fuel Classic, Calif.	TSN
4:00pm	Inside Winston Cup Racing	TNN
4:30pm R	Winners: Willy T. Ribbs	TNN
7:05pm	American Sports Cavalcade	TNN
8:30pm L	Raceday	TNN

1993 NHRA WINSTON DRAG RACING SERIES SCHEDULE
Feb. 4-7, Ponoma, Calif.; **Feb. 18-21,** Phoenix, Ariz.; **March 4-7,** Houston, Texas; **March 17-21,** Gainesville, Fla.; **April 2-4,** Rockingham, N.C.; **April 22-25,** Atlanta, Ga.; **May 13-16,** Memphis, Tenn.; **May 20-23,** Englishtown, N.J.; **June 10-13,** Columbus, Ohio; **July 9-11,** Montreal, Quebec, Canada; **July 22-25,** Denver, Colo.; **July 29-Aug. 1,** Sonoma, Calif.; **Aug. 6-8,** Seattle, Wash.; **Aug. 19-22,** Brainerd, Minn.; **Sep. 2-6,** Indianapolis, Ind.; **Sep. 16-19,** Reading, Penn.; **Sep. 30-Oct. 3,** Topeka, Kan.; **Oct. 14-17,** Dallas, Texas; **Oct. 28-31,** Pomona, Calif.

MONDAY FEBRUARY 1

■ No events scheduled at press time

■ RACING ON TV

12:30am	Winners: Willy T. Ribbs	TNN
1:00am	The Exciting World of Speed and Beauty	TNN

THURSDAY FEBRUARY 4

■ TODAY'S EVENTS

NHRA Winston Drags, Chief Winternat'ls, Pomona, Calif.

■ No racing on TV scheduled at press time

TUESDAY FEBRUARY 2

■ No events scheduled at press time

■ RACING ON TV

3:30pm	Glory Days	ESPN
6:00pm	Motoring '93	TSN

1993 SCCA OLDSMOBILE PRO SERIES SCHEDULE
May 9, Gainesville, Ga.; **May 16,** New Orleans, La.; **May 23,** Columbus, Ohio; **June 5,** Watkins Glen, N.Y.; ***June 11,** Lexington, Ohio; **July 11,** Des Moines, Iowa; **July 24,** Lime Rock, Conn.; ***Aug. 22,** Elkhart Lake, Wis.; ***Sept. 19,** TBA; **Oct. 10,** Phoenix, Ariz.
*Tentative

FRIDAY FEBRUARY 5

■ TODAY'S EVENTS

NHRA Winston Drags, Chief Winternat'ls, Pomona, Calif.

■ No racing on TV scheduled at press time

WEDNESDAY FEBRUARY 3

■ No events scheduled at press time

■ RACING ON TV

6:00pm	Motoring '93	TSN

SATURDAY FEBRUARY 6

■ TODAY'S EVENTS

NHRA Winston Drags, Chief Winternat'ls, Pomona, Calif.

■ RACING ON TV

2:00am	Secrets of Speed	ESPN
6:00am R	'92 Interstate Batteries Race, S.C. to Ca.	ESPN
9:30am	The Exciting World of Speed and Beauty	TNN
2:30pm	NHRA Today	TNN
3:00pm	Inside Winston Cup Racing	TNN
7:30pm	Speedweek's Daytona 500 Special	ESPN
8:00pm	Busch Pole Qualifying, Daytona, Fla.	ESPN
9:00pm	IMSA GTP: Rolex 24, Daytona Beach	ESPN

SUNDAY FEBRUARY 14

■ TODAY'S EVENTS

NASCAR Winston Cup, Daytona 500, Daytona Beach, Fla.
FIA World Rally, Swedish Rally

■ RACING ON TV

2:00am	This Week in NASCAR	PRIME
6:30am	Speedweek: Daytona 500 Special	ESPN
10:00am	Winners: Eddie Hill	TNN
10:30am	NHRA Today	TNN
11:00am	Inside Winston Cup Racing	TNN
11:30am L	Raceday	TNN
12:00pm	Daytona 500 Sponsored by STP	CBS
2:00pm	American Sports Cavalcade	TNN
3:25pm	Raceday Update	TNN
3:30pm	NHRA Today	TNN
4:00pm	Inside Winston Cup Racing	TNN
4:30pm R	Winners: Eddie Hill	TNN
7:00pm	Raceday Update	TNN
7:05pm	American Sports Cavalcade	TNN
8:00pm	Speedweek: Daytona 500 Special	ESPN
8:30pm L	Raceday	TNN

1993 TOYOTA ATLANTIC CHAMPIONSHIP PRELIMINARY SCHEDULE*
April 3, Phoenix, Ariz.; **April 18,** Long Beach, Calif.; **May 9,** Gainesville, Ga.; **June 5,** Milwaukee, Wis.; **June 12,** Montreal, P.Q., Canada; **June 20,** Bowmanville, Ont., Canada; **July 17,** Toronto, Ont., Canada; **Aug. 7,** Watkins Glen, N.Y.; **Aug. 15,** Trois-Rivieres, P.Q., Canada; **Aug. 28,** Vancouver, B.C., Canada; **Sep. 11,** Lexington, Ohio; **Sep. 18,** Nazareth, Pa.; **Oct. 2,** Monterey, Calif.; **Oct. 3,** Monterey, Calif.
*One additional USA date to be announced

MONDAY FEBRUARY 15

■ No events scheduled at press time

■ RACING ON TV

1:00am	The Exciting World of Speed and Beauty	TNN
3:30am	NASCAR Busch Series, Daytona	ESPN
12:30pm R	Winners: Eddie Hill	TNN
3:00pm	Speedweek: Daytona 500 Special	ESPN

THURSDAY FEBRUARY 18

■ TODAY'S EVENTS

NHRA Winston Drags, Motorcraft-Ford Nat'ls, Phoenix, Ariz.

■ RACING ON TV

3:00pm	This Week in NASCAR	PRIME
11:00pm	This Week in NASCAR	PRIME

TUESDAY FEBRUARY 16

■ No events or racing on TV scheduled at press time

1993 BRIDGESTONE SUPERCAR CHAMPIONSHIP SCHEDULE
Feb. 21, Toyota GP of Miami, Miami, Fla.; **April 18,** Atlanta Motor Speedway, Hampton, Ga.; **May 16,** GP Du Mardi Gras, New Orleans, La.; **May 31,** Lime Rock Park, Lime Rock, Conn.; **June 27,** Watkins Glen Int'l, Watkins Glen, N.Y.; **July 25,** Laguna Seca Raceway, Monterey, Calif.; **Aug. 1,** Portland Int'l Raceway, Portland, Ore.; **Sep. 5,** GP of Greater San Diego, Del Mar, Calif.; **Sep. 19,** Pontiac GP, Pontiac, Mich.; **Oct. 10,** Phoenix Int'l Raceway, Phoenix, Ariz.

FRIDAY FEBRUARY 19

■ TODAY'S EVENTS

NHRA Winston Drags, Motorcraft-Ford Nat'ls, Phoenix, Ariz.

■ RACING ON TV

10:30pm	MTEG Off-Road Championship, Anaheim	ESPN

1993 MICKEY THOMPSON STADIUM OFF-ROAD SERIES
Jan. 30, Anaheim, Calif.; **Feb. 20,** San Diego, Calif.; **March 20,** Seattle, Wash.; **May 1,** Tempe, Ariz.; **May 22,** Los Angeles, Calif.; **Sep. TBA,** Denver, Colo.; **Oct. TBA,** Las Vegas, Nev.; **Oct. TBA,** San Francisco, Calif.; **Nov. 20,** TBA.

WEDNESDAY FEBRUARY 17

■ No events scheduled at press time

■ RACING ON TV

6:00pm	Motoring '93	TSN

SATURDAY FEBRUARY 20

■ TODAY'S EVENTS

IMSA Exxon Supreme, Toyota GP of Miami, Miami, Fla.
MTEG Jack Murphy Stadium Off-Road Series, San Diego
NHRA Winston Drags, Motorcraft-Ford Nat'ls, Phoenix, Ariz.

■ RACING ON TV

2:30pm	NHRA Today	TNN
3:00pm	Inside Winston Cup Racing	TNN
3:30pm	American Sports Cavalcade	TNN

SUNDAY FEBRUARY 28

■ TODAY'S EVENTS

NASCAR Winston Cup, Goodwrench 500, Rockingham, N.C.

■ RACING ON TV

10:00am	Winners: Bobby Labonte	TNN
10:30am	NHRA Today	TNN
11:00am	Inside Winston Cup Racing	TNN
11:30am	Raceday	TNN
12:00pm L	Special: NASCAR Goodwrench 500	TNN
5:00pm	NHRA Today	TNN
5:30pm	Inside Winston Cup Racing	TNN
7:00pm	Raceday Update	TNN
7:05pm	American Sports Cavalcade	TNN
8:30pm	Raceday	TNN

1993 FORMULA 1 GRAND PRIX SCHEDULE
March 14, South African, Kyalami; **March 28,** Brazilian, Interlagos; **April 11,** European, Donington; **April 25,** San Marino, Imola; **May 9,** Spanish, Barcelona; **May 23,** Monaco, Monte Carlo; **June 13,** Canadian, Montreal; **July 4,** French, Magny-Cours; **July 11,** British, Silverstone; **July 25,** German, Hockenheim; **Aug. 15,** Hungarian, Hungaroring; **Aug. 29,** Belgian, Spa; **Sep. 12,** Italian, Monza; **Sep. 26,** Portuguese, Estoril; **Oct. 24,** Japanese, Suzuka; **Nov. 7,** Australian, Adelaide.

MONDAY MARCH 1

■ No events scheduled at press time

■ RACING ON TV

12:30am R	Winners: Bobby Labonte	TNN

THURSDAY MARCH 4

■ TODAY'S EVENTS

FIA World Rally, Portugese Rally
NHRA Winston Drags, Slick 50 Nationals, Huston, Texas

■ No racing on TV scheduled at press time

PPG CUP INDY LIGHTS
Apr. 4, Phoenix; **Apr. 18,** Long Beach; **June 6,** Milwaukee; **June 13,** Detroit; **June 27,** Portland; **July 11,** Cleveland; **July 18,** Toronto; **Aug. 8,** New Hampshire; **Aug. 29,** Vancouver; **Sep. 12 ,** Mid-Ohio; **Sep. 19,** Nazareth; **Oct. 3,** Laguna Seca.

TUESDAY MARCH 2

■ TODAY'S EVENTS

FIA World Rally, Portugese Rally

■ No racing on TV scheduled at press time

FRIDAY MARCH 5

■ TODAY'S EVENTS

FIA World Rally, Portugese Rally
NHRA Winston Drags, Slick 50 Nationals, Huston, Texas

■ No racing on TV scheduled at press time

WEDNESDAY MARCH 3

■ TODAY'S EVENTS

FIA World Rally, Portugese Rally

■ RACING ON TV

6:00pm	Motoring '93	TSN

SATURDAY MARCH 6

■ TODAY'S EVENTS

FIA World Rally, Portugese Rally
NHRA Winston Drags, Slick 50 Nationals, Huston, Texas
NASCAR Busch Grand Nat'l, Hardees 200, Richmond, Va.

■ No racing on TV scheduled at press time

1993 IMSA CAMEL GT SCHEDULE
Jan. 31, Daytona, Fla.; **Feb. 21,** Miami, Fla.; **March 30,** Sebring, Fla.; **April 18,** Atlanta, Ga.; **May 16,** New Orleans, La.; **May 31,** Lime Rock, Ct.; **June 13,** Mid-Ohio, Ohio; **June 27,** Watkins Glen, N.Y.; **July 11,** Road America, Wis.; **July 25,** Laguna Seca, Calif.; **Aug. 1,** Portland, Ore.; **Sep. 5,** San Diego, Calif.; **Sep. 19,** Pontiac, Mich.; **Sep. 26,** TBA; **Oct. 10,** Phoenix, Ariz.

All times listed are for Eastern Time Zone. Times accurate at time of printing, but check your local listings for any changes.   February 1993 *RACER* **17**

Because the major networks may broadcast programs at different times in different time zones, readers are encouraged to confirm this information with their local listings.

LOLA T93/00
Refining the Edge

■ Lola's T93/00 is the sixth Indy car designed by Bruce Ashmore since he took over as the company's Indy car design chief in 1987. Ashmore, 33, has been with Lola for 15 years, joining as an apprentice fabricator and mechanic, and earning his engineering degree in his spare time.

"The new car is a development of last year's Cosworth car," commented Ashmore about the T93/00. "Apart from the safety regulation changes at the front of the car, it looks very similar to last year's car, but it's quite different underneath. We've gotten rid of all the fit and cracking problems we had with the '92 Cosworth car, which is a usual thing when you start something from scratch."

Last year's T92/00-Ford chassis proved finicky to set up early in the year. The car was much better later in the year, once Ashmore and the Newman/Haas engineers had figured out what was wrong, and Ashmore said these lessons have been built into the T93/00.

"It was really an aerodynamic problem," he commented. "The front wings weren't a proper match with the underbody, and the rear suspension geometry wasn't quite right. The car's center of pressure was farther back than the '91 and '92 Chevy cars, and that caught me out a lot more than we thought. In the wind tunnel it's just a case of putting more front wing on and balancing it, but it's not like that on the track because it's a dynamic situation."

This year's Ford-Cosworth and Chevy/C cars are very similar, differing only in packaging details. "Same concept, just different bits to suit the bolt pattern on the two engines," noted Ashmore. "The oil tank layout is slightly different. Those kind of details.

"There's a different tail because the Chevy is a little bigger. Not in the sense that it will hurt performance-wise, it's just very slightly larger. Aerodynamically, the Chevy and Cosworth cars have the same performance in the wind tunnel, so the difference in the two should be in how they put the power down and how much horsepower each has."

No Chevy/A-powered cars had been ordered by Christmas, though Ashmore says a car could

DEVELOPMENT JOB

Applying the lessons of experience has led Lola to produce the 93/00 (ABOVE). Two basic versions of the new car were designed, one to house the Ford-Cosworth (BELOW) and Chevy/C engines, the other for the Buick V6 and Chevy/A engines. A longer, wider monocoque with full-length carbon underside increases structural rigidity and driver safety (RIGHT) while conforming to '93 rules.

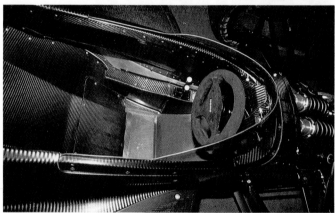

be quickly put together if any orders came in. There were four Buick V6-engined T93/00s under construction, however, all so far, for John Menard's team.

"We've put quite a lot of effort in the Buick car," said Ashmore. "Originally we thought Buick would pay for it, but since they pulled out Menard has picked up the project. Like last year, it really will be the car to run at Indianapolis if you want the pole."

This year's new chassis frontal construction rules have added some 20lb to the front of the T93/00 chassis. Material thicknesses at the front of the chassis have gone up 25 percent, and there's extra honeycomb in the nose itself. The nose is also shorter, and located much farther ahead of the driver's feet, which now rest behind a double-bulkheaded crash structure.

"The new safety rules look very sensible," commented Ashmore. "You've got 12in. of actual chassis in front of the forward bulkhead, and there will be less leverage on the nose as far as plucking it off. The nose joint looks very logical. You wouldn't have been able to do that last year, because it

wouldn't have passed the crash-test rule. They had to change the crash-test rule as far as the leverage test on the nose, but I think this arrangement is much better. It should be much safer."

By Christmas, 15 Ford-Cosworth cars had been ordered, and the first of them were ready for shipping. Ten Chevy/C-engined cars had been ordered, but the first of those won't be delivered

until the end of January.

Ashmore continues as the chief overseer of the Ford-Cosworth cars, working in the field with Newman/Haas. Buick project chief John Travis moves over to the Chevy program, working with Bernstein's team. Travis will go to the first test with Menard's cars, but then hand that project over to Graham Humphries.

—*Gordon Kirby*

AUSTRALIA INDY CAR GRAND PRIX PACKAGE

March 17-24, 1993
Gold Coast, Australia

$1299
Per Person
Sharing Twin
(Singles Add $220)

Package includes:*

- Round trip airfare from Los Angeles to Brisbane
- 6 nights accommodation at the Chevron Hotel in Surfers Paradise, Gold Coast
- Gold Reserved grandstand race seats for Saturday, March 20 and Sunday, March 21
- Entrance to Drag Racing Friday, March 19
- Entrance to Seaworld
- Transfers between the Brisbane Airport and your Gold Coast hotel

*Options available—pit passes, ball tickets and driver cocktail reception

Air taxes additional

> **• Pre- or post-Indy extensions • Car rentals • Hotel upgrades**
> **• Accommodations and sightseeing throughout Australia**

FOR RESERVATIONS OR INFORMATION HAVE YOUR TRAVEL AGENT CONTACT:

Avanti DESTINATIONS

800-422-5053

BE THERE OR WE'LL START WITHOUT YOU!